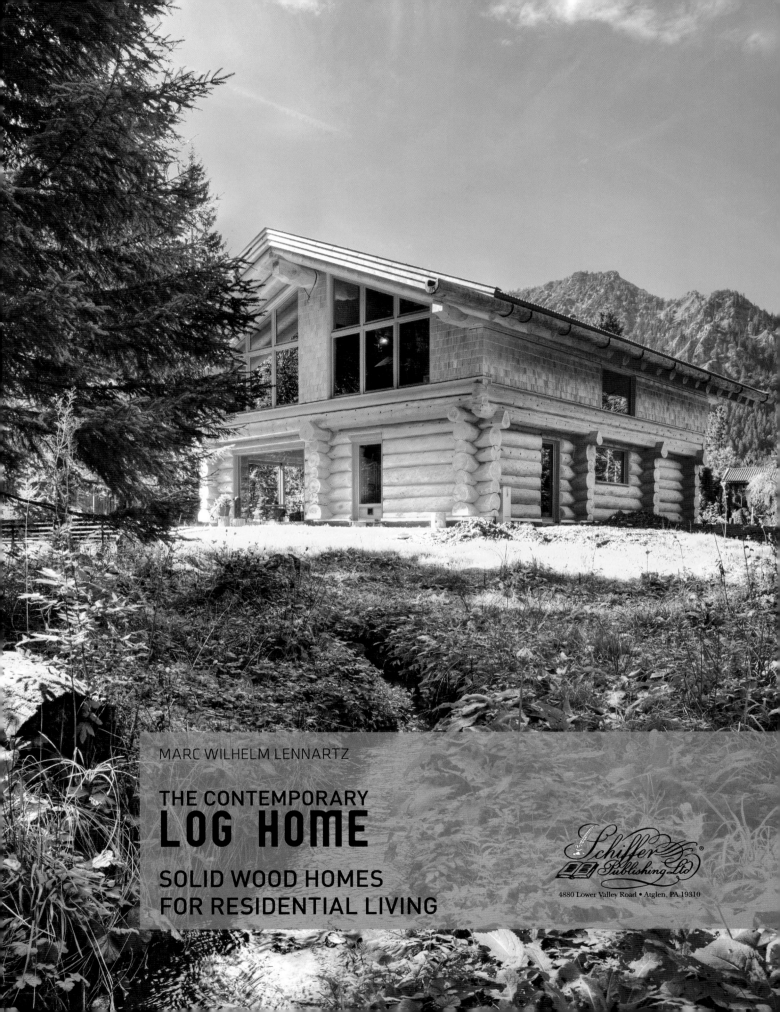

MARC WILHELM LENNARTZ

THE CONTEMPORARY
LOG HOME

SOLID WOOD HOMES
FOR RESIDENTIAL LIVING

Schiffer
Publishing Ltd

4880 Lower Valley Road • Atglen, PA 19310

MARC WILHELM LENNARTZ

THE CONTEMPORARY
LOG HOME

SOLID WOOD HOMES FOR RESIDENTIAL LIVING

CONTENTS

008   INTRODUCTION

020   FULLWOOD WOHNBLOCKHAUS GMBH
ALL OF LIFE UNDER ONE ROOF
GERMANY, LOWER RHINE

026   HOLZBAU MAIER GMBH & CO. KG
**LOG HOUSE VILLA ON THE
GROSSVENEDIGER MOUNTAIN**
AUSTRIA, PINZGAU

032   MARK MASSIVHOLZHAUS
BADEN UNION
GERMANY, KARLSRUHE

038   JOST NATURSTAMMHAUS
POST & BEAM IN THE SIEG RIVER VALLEY
GERMANY, BERGISCHES LAND

042   LOG BLOCKHAUS ING. THOMAS ZEILINGER GMBH
ON PILLARS OF LARCH AND SPRUCE
AUSTRIA, BURGENLAND

046   ELK-FERTIGHAUS AG
TUSCAN LOG HOUSE IN SPESSART
GERMANY, SPESSART

052   DAS HOLZHAUS OLIVER SCHATTAT GMBH
DREAM HOUSE FROM THE TREE OF LIFE
GERMANY, SPESSART

058   HOLZBAU ANDREAS VOLLMERS
LOG HOUSE BUNGALOW ON THE GEEST RIDGE
GERMANY, LOWER SAXONY

064   POLAR LIFE HOUSE – HONKATALOT
LOG HOUSE AMONG THE STONY PEAKS
SWITZERLAND, CANTON SCHWYZ

070   RUBNER HAUS AG
CASA BLANCA IN APULIA
ITALY, PUGLIA

076   BLOCKHAUSBAU PORRENGA GMBH
RESIDENTIAL, COMMERCIAL, AND MODEL LOG HOUSE
SWITZERLAND, CANTON ZURICH

082   FLOSS ZIMMEREI AND BLOCKHAUSBAU GMBH
MASTERPIECE IN ICHTERBERG
GERMANY, EIFEL

086   CHIEMGAU LOG HOUSE
WITH TRADITION INTO THE MODERN
GERMANY, BAVARIA

090   HONKARAKENNE OYJ
AT HOME IN NATURE
GERMANY, TAUNUS

096   ARTIFEX GMBH
**THE ART OF POST-MODERN
LOG HOUSE CONSTRUCTION**
GERMANY, BAVARIA

100   CHARLIE MANZ BLOCKHAUSBAU GMBH
A REAL PIECE OF CANADA
GERMANY, LOWER SAXONY

104 GEBRÜDER DUFTER GMBH
THREE LOG HOME BROTHERS IN THE ALPS
GERMANY, BAVARIA

108 NORDIC HAUS BLOCKHÄUSER
A SYSTEM WITH CONVICTION
GERMANY, LOWER SAXONY

112 GRAHAM BRUCE OFIELD
A CANADIAN-FRISIAN COMPOSITION
GERMANY, TECKLENBURGER LAND

118 TEAM KANADABLOCKHAUS GMBH
**LOG HOUSE IN AN ENERGY-INDEPENDENT
ALPINE COMMUNITY**
AUSTRIA, SALZBURG

124 LÖFFLER NATURSTAMMHAUS GMBH & CO. KG.
MARITIME PERSPECTIVES
GERMANY, MECKLENBURG-VORPOMMERN

130 REMS-MURR-HOLZHAUS GMBH
JEWEL ON THE PALATINATE WINE ROUTE
GERMANY, RHINELAND-PALATINATE

134 VINZENZ BACHMANN
THE TRAUNSTEIN LOG HOME TRADITION
GERMANY, BAVARIA

138 FISCHER HOLZBAU GMBH
SELF-SUFFICIENT IN EASTERN WHITE CEDAR
GERMANY, MECKLENBURG-VORPOMMERN

142 DANYS LOG HOME
SWISS PRECISION
SWITZERLAND, CANTON OF BERN

146 BERNATH+WIDMER, ARCHITEKTEN ETH HTL SIA
HARDWOOD PROTOTYPE ON THE REIAT
SWITZERLAND, CANTON OF SCHAFFHAUSEN

152 ARCHITEKT D.I. LANZINGER ANTONIUS
ONE-ROOM LOG TOWER
AUSTRIA, TYROL

158 MASSIV-HOLZ-MAUER ENTWICKLUNGS GMBH
NEW PATHS FOR WOOD HOUSES
GERMANY, BADEN-WÜRTTEMBERG

162 KONTIOTUOTE OY
DREAM LOG HOUSE OF THE ARCTIC CIRCLE
UKRAINE

166 PIONEER LOG HOMES OF BRITISH COLUMBIA
LOG HOUSE PALACE IN THE ROCKY MOUNTAINS
CANADA, BRITISH COLUMBIA

172 MANUFACTURER CONTACTS

174 COPYRIGHT AND EDITION NOTICE

5

"If we didn't have wood,
we wouldn't have fire,
we would have to eat all of our food raw
and freeze in winter,
we wouldn't have houses,
or limestone, or brick;
no glass, no metals.
We would not have tables or doors,
or chairs or any other household utensil."

—Wolf Helmhard von Hohberg,
Protestant country aristocrat and prominent writer
of the so-called German Hausväterliteratur, or household literature, genre, 1682.

INTRODUCTION

The use of solid wood for the construction of residential and commercial structures is one of the oldest building methods known to humankind. From the initially crude forms, there emerged over the millennia more and more perfect structures facilitated by diverse traditions, styles, and construction methods. This book explores the multi-faceted and wide range of modern, solid wood construction. Both the classic log house style, featuring walls made of horizontally stacked logs, naturally textured, round, or squared with overlapping corner notched joints, and the timber frame construction with its large, solid wood frame elements will constitute the focus of discussion. The crucial parameters, characteristics, and differences of the various solid wood construction methods will be presented and described in detail in the body of the book through a selection of representative properties. Moreover, great emphasis was placed on the connection between the renewable resource, wood, and the use of renewable energies, which have long since been adopted in solid wood construction.

Interglacial Period

The start of a new interglacial period, the Holocene, about 12,000 years ago, paved the way for fundamental lifestyle and economic changes, which originated in the modern-day Near East and gradually spread westward. Nomadic hunter-gatherer societies, which had formerly lived in tent-like dwellings, began to settle down and build houses. In the course of time, log house and solid wood construction evolved side-by-side with the development of settlements. Softwood trees were mainly used for construction because they were abundant and because they grew straight and relatively quickly to a suitable length. Today, there are various solid wood construction techniques: from hand-crafted construction using whole logs, or the serial manufacturing of pre-fabricated and milled timber frame elements, to the assembly-line production of computer-designed, whole wall systems.

This historical development will be illustrated by examining three selected examples

The First Stilt Houses

Wood became an essential construction material at the start of the Stone Age. Early tribal long houses with wooden frames measuring up to 131 feet [40 meters] in length can be dated back to about 8,000 years ago, when the practice of agriculture of the Linear Pottery Culture spread from the Near East toward the West. Structures of one or two stories, built with posts or ridges and pillars with walls made of a mix of wood and earth, were characteristic of early settlements. There is solid proof that both lake stilt dwellings and early log houses were already built in Central Europe in the Neolithic Period from about 4,000 BC on. Building techniques and styles differ significantly from region to region as a result of the particular varieties of wood that were available in each area. Even in those ancient times, people realized that different kinds of wood were suited for different construction purposes. For this reason, oak and

↑ Reconstruction of prehistoric stilt log houses on Lake Constance, Germany.

European silver fir were used for load-bearing posts, while long ash, hazelnut, and alder were used in the superstructure. Log houses were mostly constructed with pine.

The "Shredded" Wood Houses of the Slavs

In Niederlausitz, or Lower Lusatia, Germany, the archetype of an early log construction technique was found that can be traced back to as early as the Bronze Age about 3,500 years ago. The Slavs, who had migrated into that region from the east, starting in the early Middle Ages in the eighth century, later developed this style further, creating their own unique form of wooden architecture. Their houses made of pine logs are called Schrotholzhäuser in

↑ A Slavic Schrotholzhaus ("shredded" wood house), originally built in pine in 1713-1714, located in Saxony, Germany.

↑ Originally the Director's House, designed in 1927 by an early twentieth century pioneer of wood construction, Konrad Wachsmann; now it is the Wood Construction Information Center in Saxony, Germany.

German, or "shredded" wood houses, because of their distinctive rough-hewn look. The pine trees used for their construction were carefully selected and girdled below the tree crown three to four years before they were cut. In this process, the trees were de-barked spirally so that sap could collect in the trunk. The sap preserved the log beams that were later made from the tree and protected them from insect infestation, fungal growth, and climatic conditions. After the trees were felled, the trunks were rough hewn, chiseled, or "shredded" with a broad hand adze or axe, hence that name—Schrotholzhäuser.

Industrial Log House Construction

Konrad Wachsmann, a protagonist of the Bauhaus School, who became known throughout the world as a pioneer of industrial or prefabricated construction because of his innovative building systems, started his career in Niesky, Germany, in solid wood construction. His design for a two-story director's residence in log construction fashion was built in 1927. Conceived for functionality, this solid wood construction for the modern age features large windows and clear lines. The factory-built structure was set on top of a brick-walled basement foundation. The 2.76" [7 centimeter] thick planks were covered with additional paneling on the inside. Projecting foundation beams served as drip edges, and end-grain boards protected the saddle corners. The 59-foot-long [18-meter] log walls necessitated beam junctions. While the ceiling beams cut through the second-story exterior walls, the partition walls were inserted in a groove in the exterior wall.

Essential Features and Properties

The features and properties described in the following pages are only completely relevant and valid for solid wood structures, that is, those buildings whose components are up to ninety percent made of natural, untreated wood. These attributes will hardly, if at all, be of any benefit in those buildings that in everyday language are commonly referred to as wood houses—timber frame, stud, and skeleton structures, which may be eighty percent or more composed of insulation material. In terms of their composition, such houses should more accurately be called "insulation material constructions with wood components."

Hygroscopic Property

Wood possesses numerous tiny cavities within its cells and inter-cellular spaces. This system of cavities absorbs moisture and transports it elsewhere. Wood's hygroscopic property allows solid wood walls to absorb, store, and, in the case of overly dry conditions, to release great amounts of moisture back into a room's air. As a result, the room humidity in solid wood buildings adjusts itself to the seasons and the weather conditions, allowing people to enjoy a constantly healthy and comfortable indoor climate that is never too dry or too humid.

Sorption Ability

Sorption ability is a term that refers to the ability of natural building materials to filter gases and air pollutants. Wood's fine microstructure, porous cell walls, and integrated capillary system result in a large inner surface that in turn forms the basis for wood's high sorption capacity. Solid wood walls not only help regulate room humidity, but also help eliminate air pollutants and odors. Moreover, walls of solid wood can wick away excess moisture to the outside because of wood's natural diffusion properties. For this reason, solid

↑ Hearth and home, that is, a craftsman-built hearth and a log home: Tried and true partners for creating a good indoor climate and saving energy (Project page 124).

wood construction can create an ideal living environment for allergy sufferers, as long as they have no allergies to natural wood components.

Indoor Climate

A natural building material, wood exudes peace, harmony, and comfort, creating a very pleasant ambiance. Wood creates a healthy living environment as no other material can. Fluctuations in indoor humidity levels are corrected and kept within levels that most people would find comfortable—between thirty and fifty-five percent relative humidity throughout the year. In today's post-modern, industrial, and knowledge-based society, people spend up to ninety percent of their lives indoors. For this reason, creating a clean and natural indoor climate is of great importance for people's health. Even a little indoor pollution can have comparatively serious consequences because of the great amount of time spent indoors. Everyone should experience first-hand the indoor climate in a log or solid wood house.

Thermal Conductivity and Insulating Property

The thermal conductivity of a building material determines the degree of its insulating property—the lower the thermal conductivity, the higher the insulating property. Solid wood has the lowest thermal conductivity of all common, load-bearing building materials, which makes it a great natural insulation choice. The thermal conductivity of a brick wall structure is five factors higher than that of a solid wood wall. This means that a much thinner solid wood wall construction, taking up less construction space, can achieve the same

13

↑ Restful nights are guaranteed in this natural interior with log walls that allow free diffusion and have a high sorption capacity (Project page 52). .

↑ Saddle notch with projecting logs: Saddle-shaped notches are cut into the bottom and top logs. The lower notch of the top log rests on the upper notch of the log below it.

↑ Dovetail notch without an overhang: characteristically built with tapered log ends to ensure that the two log beams interlock securely. The trapezoid form of the log ends resembles a dove's tail.

insulation values as those of a conventional stone or brick wall. The temperatures of interior spaces and interior room surfaces (walls, floors, ceilings, windows) are what determine how warm people feel in an interior space. Wood has a high surface temperature and always feels relatively warm compared to cold, conventional stone walls. As a result, people feel comfortable in solid wood homes even at relatively low room temperatures and this can lead to more energy savings. Moreover, wood is the building material with the best ratios of insulation to thermal energy storage. An organic material, wood can store large amounts of heat for its weight and can release that heat again as needed. In this way, the wood used for construction provides an excellent thermal storage system for the entire building. This property of wood ensures that rooms cool down very slowly. Houses made of solid wood keep warm in winter and stay cool in summer.

Radiation Properties

Wood is a radiation-free, non-magnetic, sound and vibration-absorbing building material. A special attribute of solid wood houses is their ability to prevent electromagnetic waves from penetrating into the living space. The level of protection afforded depends on the thickness of the wooden walls. For example, a 13.78-inch [35-centimeter] thick, solid wood wall would be needed to prevent ninety-five percent of the electromagnetic radiation emitted by mobile communications antennas from penetrating into a house. In addition, wood is electrically neutral—it does not influence or amplify electric fields or waves in any way.

Fire Safety

Modern wood constructions fully comply with fire safety regulations. When wood burns, it burns in a predictable manner, slowly, evenly and controllably. Before wood collapses, there are clear warnings; whereas, steel constructions can collapse suddenly and without warning. Wood carbonizes on the surface, thus protecting its inner structure from destruction as the carbonated layer produces a natural insulating effect that slows the rise in temperature. In this way, solid wood constructions remain intact and load bearing for a relatively long time. Insurance premiums reflect these considerations as premiums for solid wood houses are the same as those for conventional stone houses. Moreover, large, solid wood building elements, such as massive log beams, round log walling, or whole natural trunks are much less flammable than smaller building components. The thicker the wood component, the more slowly the temperature will rise on the side not facing the fire. For this reason, fire ratings rise in conjunction with the wall thickness. In Germany, for instance, the fire protection requirements specified by law call for a 30 minute fire rating (F 30 B) for load-bearing, structural elements in single-family and two-family homes. This means that a building must be able to withstand a fire for at least thirty minutes. Solid wood constructions and log houses generally have a fire rating of sixty to ninety minutes (F 60 to F90).

Wood Protection

Wood constructions that are expertly planned and crafted on the basis of years of tradition and experience do not need added chemical wood preservation. Through preventative construction measures, moisture—wood damage factor number one—can be repelled. Frost, heat, corrosion, and pollutants cannot damage wood; direct sunlight turns wood gray but does not harm it. Constructive wood protection begins with the expertise in choosing the right types of wood and the right time to harvest it, that is, in winter in the phase just before new moon. This so-called moon phase wood is wood from trees that are felled according to the silvicultural moon calendar. Wood harvested in this tradition is said to be of particularly high quality in regards to its stability, durability, hardness, and resistance to insect infestation. Up until the nineteenth century, almost all wood was felled in winter, not only in Europe but also on other continents. There is generally less sap in tree trunks in the winter and the wood felled at that time is drier. In addition, the sap moves toward the roots of trees in the period of the waning moon, with the result that the diameter of the trunk shrinks a little. The special properties of such wood depend not only on the right choice for the time of felling, but also on the right choices for the method of storing and drying the wood, right up to its careful processing, which is far from hasty mass production methods. Significant, protective construction measures include the use of dry, weather-resistant wood types, the securing of permanent ventilation for wood, the prevention of water build-up, and the use of wide roof overhangs and steeply pitched roofs that extend far down. Projecting wooden components are equipped with drip edges that will ensure that any rainwater and other moisture will drip down away from the structure. In addition, the ground sill should be a safe distance from the ground surface in order to protect the building from splashing water in heavy downfalls.

Light-weight, Dry and Flexible Construction

Wood, though relatively light in weight, has a high load bearing capacity. Wood's low overall weight makes it possible to build not only smaller, less expensive foundations but also thinner wall constructions since the entire thickness of the solid log walls functions as a layer of natural insulation. In addition, wood has a long fatigue limit, is elastic, but at the same time, unbreakable. Because of this, wood construction is used all over the world since building components made of elastic wood can absorb both vertical and horizontal forces, and can even compensate for them to a certain degree. For this reason, solid wood houses are much more earthquake resistant than rigid stone constructions. Moreover, the construction problems caused by moisture no longer need to be taken into consideration. If dried wood is used, rooms can be inhabited as soon as they are built. This dry construction method with wood as the building material, which allows free diffusion, also prevents mold. This results in lasting benefits to the health not only of the inhabitants but also of the construction. Furthermore, building with wood allows a great degree of flexibility in regard to floor plans, room layouts, and appointments, as well as later extensions and remodeling. Combining wood with other materials, such as glass, natural stone, or clay, or even steel and concrete, is easy and affords immense freedom in planning and design possibilities. In addition, many types of solid wood constructions can be extensively prefabricated so that a period of four to six months should generally be sufficient to complete construction, including interior work.

Energy, Ecology, and Climate Protection
Energy Footprint

The small energy footprint of solid wood and log buildings is unparalleled: The production, transportation, use, maintenance, and recycling of these structures demand much less energy than that of all other building types. The greatest energy consumption occurs during the production process of building materials. Other important factors, such as durability and recyclability, play a significant role in the energy equation as well. According to Germany's Federal Environmental Agency, the natural building material wood requires 8 to 30 kWh/m3 (8 to 30 kilowatt hours per cubic meter or per 35.31 cubic feet or 1.31 cubic yards) for its production, transportation, and processing. In comparison, concrete requires 150 to 200 kWh/m3, and steel building components 500 to 600 kWh/m3. Trees don't need fossil fuels to grow and they take more CO_2 out of the atmosphere while they are growing than they later put into the atmosphere while they are being processed into construction timber, sawn lumber, and wood-based materials. As a result, houses made of solid wood require many times less fossil energy for their production as do conventional stone or brick constructions or even passive, low-energy, and energy-plus houses, which are built mainly of insulation materials. Insulation materials use lots of energy, require additional transport, and call for high energy and logistical costs in the processing and production chain. In addition, the untreated wood used in solid wood construction can, even after having served one purpose for at least 100 years, be used again to provide new

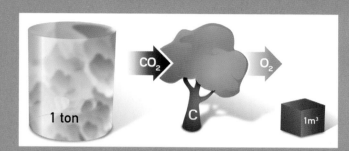

↑ In 1m3 of wood, one ton of CO2 (carbon dioxide) is stored during the process of photosynthesis.

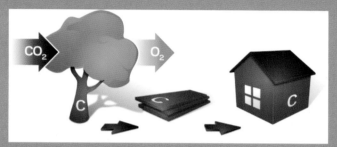

↑ Through the production of durable goods made of solid wood, carbon dioxide (CO2) is taken out of the atmosphere—an example of active climate protection.

log buildings with warm water and heat. Thus, the energy produced by solid wood surpasses many times over the energy originally needed to produce the material—a perfect cycle unique to solid wood construction. Moreover, when wood is burned, it only releases as much carbon dioxide into the atmosphere as the tree took out of the atmosphere during its growth. Proof of the exemplary environmental consciousness in solid-wood construction circles is the fact that highly efficient fireplaces, tiled or soapstone masonry heaters, as well as pellet, wood chip, or wood stoves are installed in most solid wood and log homes. Those who heat with wood are active practitioners of climate and environmental protection. Even the ashes can be used as an environmentally friendly fertilizer in the garden.

Sustainability Through Use

For the most part, forestry in Europe has followed the principle of sustainability for more than 250 years: only as much wood is cut as can grow back naturally or be reforested. At present, the annual growth of usable wood in Europe is greater than the amount logged. Total utilization could be increased by about a third. Furthermore, this valuable natural resource almost always grows in or near the area of its final use. Yet, even when transportation costs are involved, they do not take a large toll on the bottom line since wood is relatively light-weight. In old-growth forests, which enjoy special protective status because of their biodiversity, as well as in the specially protected forests of national parks, there is no logging. Such places, in which there is a balance between the absorption and the release of carbon dioxide, act as fully utilized carbon reservoirs. Only sustainable forest husbandry, that considers wood in the form of durable wood products as part of an overall carbon strategy, can have an even greater positive impact.

Durable wood products bind carbon more effectively than the carbon cycle of the virgin forests can do alone. Harvested wood in the form of wood products, in fact, extends the carbon storage effect of forests for decades, thereby increasing the forests' storage capacities. At the same time, through regular reforestation, more CO2 is taken out of the atmosphere with the growth of young trees. An increase in the use of wood is not harmful to the forest ecosystem, but beneficial: sustainable forestry leads to periodic regeneration and, as a consequence, to better structure and greater stability of the forests. Wood, in turn, replaces fossil fuels (oil, gas, coal) and materials produced with energy-intensive processes, thereby eliminating their CO_2 emissions. On average, each cubic meter of wood that is substituted for other building materials reduces the CO_2 emissions in the atmosphere by one ton. If this ton is added to the ton of CO_2 that is already stored within the wood, then one can say that every cubic meter of wood used for construction eliminates about two tons of CO_2. As the great number of historical wood buildings still in existence today can attest, log and solid wood houses are the champions of carbon storage capacity—extremely durable goods made of solid wood that can last for centuries. In that amount of time, generations of spruce, pine, fir, Douglas fir, larch, Western Red and Eastern White cedar, beech, and oak trees can easily grow again for log and solid wood construction. In this way, every solid wood house makes a significant contribution toward maintaining the ecological balance, saving the forests, creating a healthy climate, and in general actively supporting environmental protection.

Carbon Storage
In the age of man-made climate change as a result of greenhouse gas emissions, wood's significance as a carbon storage option is growing enormously.

Carbon dioxide, which exists in great quantities, is largely (more than 50%) to blame for causing the man-made greenhouse effect. However, through the process of photosynthesis, carbon dioxide (CO_2) is split and thus removed from the atmosphere. The harmless carbon is stored in wood and the oxygen is released into the atmosphere. Wood is the only building material that grows naturally. To grow, wood only needs sun, air, water, and earth, as well as time. The formula used to calculate the carbon storage capacity of the houses in this book is based on the explanation of Dr. Arno Frühwald from the Center of Wood Science at the University of Hamburg, Germany. He explains:

"In every cubic meter of wood, the carbon from one ton of carbon dioxide is stored through the process of photosynthesis. How much carbon dioxide is stored in one individual wood house depends on the amount of wood used for construction and therefore varies from building to building. Wood is 50% carbon (C). Based on an average value of 500 kg [1100 lbs] of wood per cubic meter [three cubic feet], one cubic meter [three cubic feet] of wood would contain 250 kg [550 lbs] of carbon. If carbon is changed into carbon dioxide, or oxidized, approximately 3.667 kg [8.084 lbs] of CO_2 are produced from 0.9 kg [1.9 lbs] of carbon. That means that the 250 kg [550 lbs] of carbon per cubic meter [three cubic feet] of wood multiplied by 3.667 kg [8.084 lbs] of carbon dioxide produce 916 kg [2019 lbs], that is, approximately one ton of carbon dioxide per one cubic meter [three cubic feet] of wood."

↑ The combination of the renewable natural resource, wood, and renewable energies in log and solid wood construction provides today's most sustainable and healthy construction choice.

Summary and Forecast

The tradition of solid wood construction, alive for thousands of years, holds an incomparable wealth of architectural, construction, and forestry experience. For over 8,000 years, people have used wood, an almost magically multifunctional material that can be used for construction, for the production of goods, and for providing energy. Solid wood construction, including both heavy full-wood construction and lightweight construction, offers many advantages. The modern solid wood house or log house fulfills all of today's legal requirements for structural engineering, construction physics, moisture protection, sound-proofing, and fire protection. The high level of craftsmanship and technical skill in solid wood construction guarantees a building's durability. With their outstanding, natural insulating qualities, wood homes will remain viable and valuable for years to come, even in times of rising energy costs. Prerequisites for long years of use and enjoyment, however, are expert planning and an experienced solid wood construction company. The combination of the renewable natural resource, wood, and the use of renewable energies—described in this book through real construction case studies spanning the full spectrum of options—sets the benchmarks for sustainable construction. In a holistic approach to weighing the environmental value of various construction methods—that is, one that takes into consideration various factors that make up the whole, such as energy balance, thermal insulation, material and resource budgeting, interior air quality and living environment, water use, climatic impact, environmental protection, ecology, construction and building processes, as well as sustainable forestry—solid wood construction takes first place with the sum of its many environmentally friendly parts. As long as there are people and forests, there will be houses built of solid wood—for all the right reasons, with lots of good experience, with a clear conscience, and with incomparable style and a real sense of living the good life naturally. ●

ALL OF LIFE UNDER ONE ROOF

Room for living, working, and relaxing—a log house made of northern pine brings separate spheres of life into harmonious interaction.

Just one look is all it takes to be captivated by the clean lines of this solid wood home. The design is consistent in its clarity, perfect in every detail, and completely free of superfluous flourishes and fussiness. This log home gets right to the point, which is the solid wood form of the pine log and its light-catching finish.

Detailed Pre-planning and Wall Elements without Settling

Two full stories offer a total of 2,648 square feet [246m2] of living space. Deliberately planned without a basement, the two-car garage located in front of the house provides ample storage space, in addition to the separate store room. The log home was constructed quickly using the manufacturer's very own prefabricated wall element system. This single-layered log house built with 7.87" [20 cm] thick, triple-bonded northern pine is impressive with its non-settling construction technique, in which the resistant heartwood forms the exterior wall. Because of this, the wall elements, thoroughly planned with computer aided design (CAD) programs, can be easily combined with other materials, for instance, brick work. The strong, asymmetric saddle-back roof has built-in weather protection with its 47.24" [1.20 meter] overhangs on gables and eaves.

Fluid Layout

The underlying design concept of the house is immediately clear to anyone who enters. The foyer is multifunctional

← Perfect in form and structure, the architect's log house known as "Reichenwald House" is making quite an impression on future home-builders.

and acts as a transitional space between the living space and the formally detached office area. Two additional, separate entries to the office and the children's room help maintain privacy, as needed. The gabled side faces south with a view of the garden from its generously sized windows that extend to the roof ridge in strict symmetry. In addition, full-length terrace windows, a gable roof, two dormers, and many large windows located throughout the house fill the interior space with light and sun.

Rest and Relaxation Inside and Out

The hub of family life is the 700-square-foot [65-square-meter] living and dining area on the first floor. The living room, with its centrally located tiled fireplace/wood oven, features a full wall of windows with a view of the garden and an open gallery above with exposed roof ridges. Along with the gallery on the second floor, there are three bedrooms, two bathrooms, and a storage room. The overall architectural composition lets the outdoors become a natural extension of the indoors—a stroll through the terrace doors into the park-like garden on the same level shows how the natural wood of the home gives way to the natural beauty of the garden. The log house's strict geometry is intentionally countered by the curved lines of the garden. A semicircular brick path leads to the Finnish open-air sauna. After a dip in the sauna, a swim in the home's own pond can be refreshing. The fun goes on under a roof canopy whimsically shaped like half of an igloo, where a whirlpool awaits its guests.

Cultivated Accents

The color and lighting décor deserve particular mention: the royal blue window and door frames of the home's exterior make a stylish contrast to the vibrant red accents of the interior. The light-colored, natural stone tile floors exude a sense of calm and gently reflect the light falling into the room. Skillful lighting techniques provided by a

← From the living area, solid wood stairs with glass parapets rise to the gallery on the second floor where the bedrooms are also located.

→ Striking and functional, the east-facing main entrance with gabled roof.

← The log house, with its Finnish sauna, swimming pond, and whirlpool, offers an outdoor lifestyle in close touch with nature.

specialized firm put the gallery, the triangular dormer, and the glass stair parapets with their stainless steel railings in the best light. This home succeeds in exuding tranquil comfort as it stirs up the senses. Heat and hot water are provided by a fully automatic wood pellet oven, which is stored in the low-energy floor heating system on both floors.

N ◑ SITE PLAN

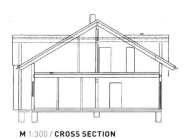

M 1:300 / **CROSS SECTION**

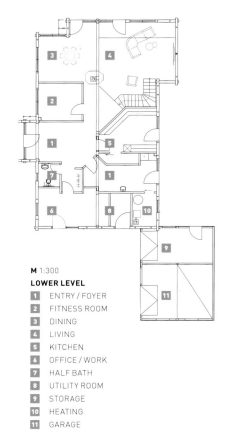

M 1:300
LOWER LEVEL
1. ENTRY / FOYER
2. FITNESS ROOM
3. DINING
4. LIVING
5. KITCHEN
6. OFFICE / WORK
7. HALF BATH
8. UTILITY ROOM
9. STORAGE
10. HEATING
11. GARAGE

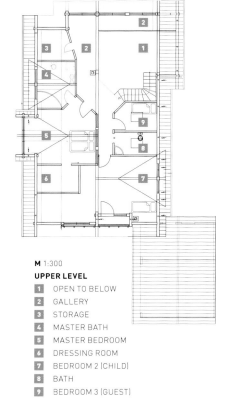

M 1:300
UPPER LEVEL
1. OPEN TO BELOW
2. GALLERY
3. STORAGE
4. MASTER BATH
5. MASTER BEDROOM
6. DRESSING ROOM
7. BEDROOM 2 (CHILD)
8. BATH
9. BEDROOM 3 (GUEST)

MANUFACTURER + ARCHITECT   FULLWOOD WOHNBLOCKHAUS GMBH
LOCATION   GERMANY, LOWER RHINE
LOT SIZE   12,906 FT² [1,199 M²]
LIVING AREA   2,648 FT² [246 M²]
BUILDING COSTS   NOT SPECIFIED
YEAR OF COMPLETION   2005

i A total of approximately **2,295 ft³ [65 m³]** of wood volume was used in construction. This is equivalent to a carbon component in wood of **17.9 tons US [16.2 metric tons]**, which is equivalent, in turn, to the storage of **66.6 tons [59.5 metric tons]** of carbon dioxide for 100 years.

↗ The gallery level, flooded with light, shows the spaciousness of the compact wood construction made of northern pine.

→ The central tiled fireplace, with its curved window, provides a 270° view of the fire—all the way from the dining room to the staircase.

LOG HOUSE VILLA ON THE GROSSVENEDIGER MOUNTAIN

In view of lofty 9,800 foot [3,000 meter] peaks, a log house in Austria's Pinzgau region upholds tradition and reveals once more the timelessness of the carpenter's skill.

Located in the central Alps of Austria, Pinzgau is a cultural region with an agrarian tradition and a long history. Southwest of Salzburg, Pinzgau is bordered to the north by the Kitzbühel Alps in Austria and Germany's Steinernes Meer, and to the south by South Tyrol, Tyrol, and Carinthia. The name, Pinzgau, comes from the bulrush plants that grew along the Salzach River banks long ago and were used to make baskets, shoes, bags, and fish traps.

Burnt and Washed for Eternity

About 3,000 feet [900 meters] above sea level, this log house villa is nestled on a southern slope steps away from a high forest. Constructed of the region's solid mountain spruce, the log house combines tried and true traditions with timeless modern elements. The spruce planks were burned and washed on their exterior side before they were installed. This process produces a fine, bright, light-brown luster while it also preserves the wood. Because of this finishing process, the exterior wooden walls will never need to be treated or painted again. The two south-facing balconies, and their decorative plank woodwork, are protected all year round under the front gable of the roof with its wide overhang. The windows of weatherproof larch complete the overall design composition based on lasting quality. The bell tower that crowns the roof ridge is reminiscent of the time when the tolling of the bell called people together to share their midday meal.

Garden as Work of Art

The 7,535 ft2 [700 m2] lot is surrounded by striking natural rock groupings. Single, distinctive stones stand alone in the garden like works of sculpture and continue the design concept of the log house villa outdoors. The solid wood spruce log house rests on a stone basement foundation and offers an impressive 2,368 ft2 [220 square meters] of living space on three stories. The eye-catching saddle notches were finished in the Pinzgau wood construction tradition in the Tyrolean palace style. Log walls 4.7" [12 cm] thick created from squared off logs are covered with a 5.5" [14-cm] thick layer of insulation made of permeable wood fiber, which is paneled on the interior with reclaimed wood.

Complete Comfort

On the basement level, the architect has created a generous space for rest and relaxation with a Finnish sauna, whirlpool, and large area for doing absolutely nothing. The storeroom and utility/mechanical room are also located on the basement level. The spacious, combined kitchen, dining, and living area on the first floor leaves nothing to be desired. A double-sided fireplace insert between the living area and the kitchen spreads its pleasant warmth throughout the space. In addition, the guest bathroom and another small room are located on the first floor. Next to the generously proportioned bedroom on the second floor is a natural stone bath with a rainforest shower. The gallery and a second bedroom complete the upper level.

→ A master craftsman's log house that shows a true eye for detail. The two south-facing balconies, with their decorative, wooden planks, are protected from the weather by the wide roof overhang.

The Interplay of Light and View

The fundamental concept of this design is based on transparency and the visual integration of the surrounding alpine panorama. Every room in the house offers wonderful views of the Grossvenediger mountains or the main ridge of the Hohe Tauern mountains. The living room and its open upper gallery level, in particular, were built to highlight the beauty of the surroundings. The west side of the house features a large wall of glass that looks onto the outdoor terrace and beyond that onto the 12,054-foot-high [3,674 meter] Grossvenediger mountain. All of the woodwork, including window shutters, stairs, and banisters were hand-made.

Geothermal Radiant Floor Heating

The exemplary planning and execution of this log house is carried through to the very last detail in the home's energy balance. A geothermal, or ground source, heat pump with a deep bore hole feeds the home's low-energy floor heating on three levels and heats its water. The use of an emissions-free geothermal heating system and the renewable natural resource of wood in this solid wood villa help create a shining example of an ecological construction that can also be cited as a real-life example of successful home design. This combination is unique in modern architecture and is breaking new ground in the realm of modern log house construction.●

29

↑ The expansive glass wall on the home's west side provides a great view of the Grossvenediger mountain, or "her age-old majesty" as the snowy main peak of the Venediger mountains is known throughout the region.

↖ The Finnish sauna, next to the family room with its wall of natural stone, offers pure relaxation in the basement level.

← Life is lived between the ceiling of reclaimed wood and the brushed oak floor boards. The double-sided, free-standing fireplace serves as a room divider between the living and eating areas.

→ Tried and true for centuries, the beautiful "Tiroler-Schloss" notch.

M 1:300
SECOND FLOOR
1 OPEN TO ROOM BELOW
2 GALLERY
3 STORAGE
4 BEDROOM
5 BATH
6 BALCONY

M 1:300
FIRST FLOOR
1 ENTRY
2 LAUNDRY
3 HALF BATH
4 STORAGE
5 LIVING
6 DINING
7 KITCHEN
8 TERRACE
9 BALCONY

M 1:300 / **CROSS SECTION**

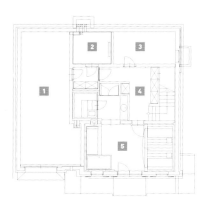

M 1:300
BASEMENT LEVEL
1 GARAGE
2 UTILITY
3 CELLAR
4 ANTEROOM
5 SAUNA

M 1:300/ **EAST ELEVATION**

MANUFACTURER	HOLZBAU MAIER GMBH & CO. KG
ARCHITECT	PETER NIEDEREGGER
LOCATION	AUSTRIA, PINZGAU
LOT SIZE	700 M² (7,535 FT²)
LIVING AREA	220 M² (2,368 FT²)
CONSTRUCTION COSTS	NOT SPECIFIED
COMPLETION	2008

 A total of approximately **6,710 ft³ [190 m³]** of wood was used in construction. This is equivalent to a carbon component in wood of **52.36 tons [47.5 metric tons]**, which is equivalent, in turn, to the storage of **195.55 tons [191.8 metric tons]** of carbon dioxide for 100 years.

↗ Restful nights in natural solid wood surroundings.

→ Leaving nothing to be desired: luxurious kitchen ambiance combined with an exclusive view.

BADEN UNION

Long ago in the German state of Baden-Württemberg, the Margraves reigned in Karlsruhe, the "sun fan city"— famous for the fan-like shape of its streets, which radiate out from the center. Today a union of ecological construction skill and wood construction expertise reign in this modern log house in Karlsruhe.

The log house, built with high mountain spruce that was felled in the winter, was planned without a basement level, and was completed and ready for occupancy after only four months of construction. Design details such as the wooden beam ceilings or the Tyrolean style log wall notches are easy to notice. Other well-considered construction details lie below the surface, hidden to the eye. The multi-layered wall construction with its interior log plank walls and exterior layer of insulation was designed to be permeable and moisture-regulating in accordance with construction physics and ecologically viable building criteria. The 4.3" [11 cm] thick spruce log planks are covered with a convection protective board. On top of that layer on the outside, there is a wooden frame construction with natural wood-fiber insulation, followed by a windproof wood fiber board, including a back ventilation layer, in which both capillary and convection moisture can dry out continuously.

Ideal Indoor Climate in a Wooden Structure

Wood's natural, hygroscopic property allows log walls to absorb a large amount of moisture from the room's air, store it and release it again into the room. The result is that indoor humidity adjusts itself ideally to the season and the current weather conditions. Home owners enjoy living in a constantly healthy and comfortable indoor cli-

↖ The exterior does not reveal how large the home is.

← A unique touch: the canted corner of the blue varnished spruce log house.

mate, which is never too dry or too humid. Even the floors were built using a consistently ecologically-minded dry construction method. A wooden floor plate was placed on a well-ventilated strip foundation made of steel-free concrete. Then wood fiber boards were laid to provide sound insulation, on top of which, in turn, large ceramic tiles were installed, providing not only an alternative to a cast plaster floor but also a material base on which to place integrated radiant floor heating. The heating pipes that run directly under the flooring provide a loss-free supply of radiant heat. In addition, the tiles with their grooves turned upward increase the radiant heating surface facing the flooring by approximately sixty percent. As a result, this type of surface heating only needs an energy-saving, low start-up temperature of about 73° to 81° Fahrenheit [23 to 27 degrees Celsius]. Finally, an oiled wood floor of Douglas fir was installed over all the layers.

A Basic Masonry Heater

A centrally located thermal storage furnace with a brick-lined combustion chamber and flues made by an expert furnace and stove maker supplies this spacious log house with comfortable radiant heat. With an efficiency of about 5 kilowatts, the furnace provides about ninety percent of the home's heating need. In addition, only about 8.8 to 11 cord feet [4 to 5 solid cubic meters] of hardwood are needed to heat the home—depending on the harshness of the winter. Because so much of the first floor is open to the second story and gallery above, the rising warmth from the first floor can heat the upper floor sufficiently. To ensure heat at peak load times, a gas condensing combi boiler on the first floor runs the low-energy radiant floor heating system. A solar thermal energy system with a collector surface of just 53.8 ft2 [5 square meters] is installed on the roof to heat water and feed a 79 gallon [300-liter] hot water tank.

← The central thermal storage heater provides healthy radiant heat for the first and second stories.

↓ Facing the evening sun: a wrap-around porch with a pergola highlights the transition from the log house to the herb garden.

→ On the unprotected parts of the roof overhang, the spruce wood forms a gray film that is structurally quite harmless.

→ Every corner of this natural, solid wood house radiates comfort and warmth.

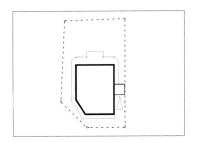

Free Log House World

The reddish-brown of the clay tiles on the pitched roof and the cerulean blue paint on the home's spruce exterior, treated with an open-pore linseed oil varnish with plant extracts that act as a UV filter, set a friendly tone. On the inside, gridded windows set around the house let light and warmth stream into the home. The first floor provides lots of room for a combined living and dining room, the kitchen, bath, half-bath, and three bedrooms. The upper floor, which has no partition walls, offers a comfortable space to read and study, as well as a seamlessly integrated sleeping loft. ●

M 1:300
MAIN LEVEL

1 ENTRY
2 BEDROOM
3 DINING
4 LIVING
5 KITCHEN
6 BATH
7 HALF-BATH
8 TERRACE

M 1:300
UPPER LEVEL

1 READING
2 BEDROOM
3 ATTIC
4 OPEN TO BELOW

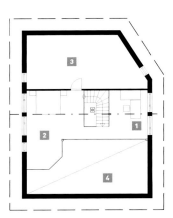

M 1:300 / **CROSS SECTION**

ℹ A total of approximately **624 ft³ [58 m³]** of wood volume was used in construction. This is equivalent to a carbon component in wood of **16 tons [14.5 metric tons]**, which is equivalent, in turn, to the storage of **58.42 tons [53 metric tons]** of carbon dioxide for 100 years.

MANUFACTURER	MARK MASSIVHOLZHAUS
ARCHITECT	BAUBIOLOGISCHES PLANUNGSBÜRO MARK & LORANG
LOCATION	GERMANY, KARLSRUHE
LOT SIZE	5,081 FT² [472 M²]
LIVING AREA	1,938 FT² [180 M²]
COST	APPROX. $448,000 [320,000 EURO] BASE OF CALCULATION: 1 EURO = $1.40 USD
COMPLETION	2008

↑ View of the living and dining area from the sleeping loft above.

POST AND BEAM IN THE SIEG RIVER VALLEY

Hard basalt stone from the depths of the earth and mature trunk wood from deep, virgin forests combine the powers of nature in this log house.

The Bergisches Land Nature Reserve [Naturpark Bergisches Land], a nature reserve located in the German state of North Rhine-Westphalia, was carved out of the northern part of the Rhenish Uplands on the right bank of the Rhine. This rainy and snowy upland region is full of rolling hills, meadows, woods, deep valleys, and countless streams. On the southern border of the nature park lies the so-called "Windeck Countryside" ["Windecker Ländchen"], a recreation area that spans the right and left banks of the meandering river Sieg and stretches up to the wooded hilltops along the edge of the valley. In the middle of this perfect, pastoral setting stands a magnificent natural log home designed with modern post and beam elements.

A Close Relation of Half-timbered or Timber Frame Construction

A post and beam construction uses heavy, solid wooden posts and beams, but employs framework, brickwork, or roundwood for partition walls. Because of this, it is a variation of classical half-timbered construction, but enhanced by the addition of details from the Canadian roundwood construction technique. This building method makes it possible to combine solid wood architecture with elements of modern style. The log house was built with untreated, round logs of high forest spruce, with an average diameter of approximately 17.7" [45 cm]. Particularly resistant Douglas fir wood was selected for the sill logs, the first layer of beams to be placed on the stone cellar foundation. Approximately 150 tons of large, gray-blue basalt blocks are piled around the foundation.

Year-round Outdoor Enjoyment

With a full basement foundation, the log house was erected on a gentle slope with a view of the Sieg river valley. An attached two-car garage was built by extending the seventh and eighth rows of logs in the house structure so that they intercept and are supported by an adjoining post construction. An overhanging porch shelters the entrance to the home, as glass doors in the vestibule lead into the open-concept living area. The practical and compact kitchen is accessed through a wonderful archway. The unique, tiled wood-burning stove fireplace, erected by a master stove builder, is the center of the living room. Tucked away under the extended wooden structure formed by the upper rows of logs, the covered porch and outdoor sitting area can be enjoyed in any weather and is accessible from both the living and dining areas. Directly adjacent to the porch is a large, south-facing wrap-around Douglas fir terrace-like balcony supported by massive trunk logs.

The Work of a Master Craftsman

A custom-built, L-shaped log staircase, also constructed of Douglas fir, leads to the upper level. Located on this level are the gallery, two bedrooms, a separate dressing area, the owner's game hunting room, and an opulent bath. Under Stefan Jost's expert supervision, the ceilings were installed throughout with roundwood beams as open rafters, which lend each and every room character and contour. Three round, natural log ridges, two middle purlins, and visible inferior purlins constitute the crossing piers of this master-crafted roof construction.

Geothermal Heat Through Surface Collectors

This natural log house is crowned with a red-brown tile roof insulated with rafter panels. Within the home's own building lot, 3,281 feet [one thousand meters] of piping for the thermal collectors was laid horizontally in big loops a

→ The wide roof overhangs protect the natural trunk log house walls made of wood from the high spruce forest..

↑ This unique, natural stone fireplace, together with an integrated heat bank and wood storage, is at the heart of the living room.

little below the ground frost depth. No permit or official approval is needed for this type of geothermal energy system. A low-energy radiant floor heating system, which is fed by the geothermal heat pump, was installed on all floors. This provides this log house—built for healthy living—with emissions-free heat and hot water year round. ●

MANUFACTURER	JOST NATURSTAMMHAUS
ARCHITECT	HELMUT RABBICH
LOCATION	GERMANY, BERGISCHES LAND
LOT SIZE	32,615 FT² [3,030 M²]
LIVING AREA	2,583 FT² [240 M²]
CONSTRUCTION COST	APPROX. $630,000 [450,000 EURO]
	BASE OF CALCULATION: 1 EURO = $1.40 USD
COMPLETION	2007

ℹ A total of approximately **2,551 ft³ [237 m³]** of wood volume was used in construction. This is equivalent to a carbon component in wood of **65.31 tons [59.25 metric tons]**, which is equivalent, in turn, to the storage of **239.2 tons [217 metric tons]** of carbon dioxide for 100 years.

M 1:300 / **FRONT ELEVATION**

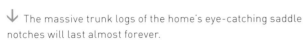

M 1:300
LOWER LEVEL
1 ENTRY
2 CLOSET
3 HALF BATH
4 KITCHEN
5 DINING
6 LIVING
7 COVERED PORCH
8 BALCONY
9 STORAGE
10 GARAGE

M 1:300
UPPER LEVEL
1 GALLERY
2 BEDROOM
3 GAME HUNTING ROOM
4 BATH
5 DRESSING ROOM / WALK-IN CLOSET
6 BALCONY

↓ The massive trunk logs of the home's eye-catching saddle notches will last almost forever.

↓ Sheltered from the weather all year round by the deep overhang of the gable roof, the balcony and the entry way are located next to the two-car garage, also executed in log house style.

ON PILLARS OF LARCH AND SPRUCE

In the northern part of the Austrian province, Burgenland, near the border to the neighboring province of Lower Austria, a log house reveals historical ties to the earliest settlements of this region.

The Leitha Mountains, a range of wooded hills about 1,476 feet [450 meters] above sea level, form the southeastern edge of the Vienna basin. In this spot, the foothills of the eastern Central Alps converge with the foothills of the northern Carpathian Mountains. In a small, rural community on the western edge of this range of hills stands a single-walled log house with a well-conceived construction system.

High and Dry
In form and execution, the log home takes its cues from historical lake dwellings built on stilts or piles, which were the early precursors of log houses. At first sight, the solid wood log house seems to be floating above the ground. The distance between the base plate and the ground varies between 13.8" to 29.5" [35 and 75 centimeters], since the house was built on a gentle slope. Because the construction under the house also creates non-stop ventilation, the material components of the structure stay dry and the wood is protected from moisture, as well as fungal growth and pest infestation. The construction is mounted on sixteen strong concrete pillars, which, in turn, are mounted on the strip foundation that is cemented into the ground. A timber beam construction made of spruce wood was placed on top of this base. The timber structure consists of 7" x 6" [18 x 15 cm] cant beams, .8" [2 cm] of planking, 2" [5 cm] of fill, covered by subfloor / dry floor screed, followed by a final component of sheetrock with integrated radiant floor heating.

Multiple Benefits
An eight-inch-thick [20-cm-thick] layer of wool insulation was installed in the structure's hollow space. The single-wall log wall system is made of multi-ply laminated beams consisting of five bonded solid wood lamellas measuring a total of 7" [18 cm]. Four layers of spruce wood totaling 6" [15 cm] are topped by one final exterior layer of larch. Relatively hard, very stable, and heavy larch wood, with its high sap content, is an extremely weatherproof exterior cladding that can be exposed to outdoor conditions, which constantly fluctuate between sun, rain, or snow.

Well-planned Small House Concept
Home owners enjoy the warm, light tones of the spruce wood interior. Another benefit gained by building the wall with multi-ply log beams is the fact that the beams were produced with dried, or cured, woods, which almost eliminate the structural engineering problems caused by settling. The lower level features an open-concept living and dining area with a gallery and a view of the south-facing garden, as well as a large kitchen with a pantry. An office/work room, a large bath, a half-bath, and a storage room are also located on the first floor. The upper level contains, apart from the gallery, the master bedroom with a walk-in closet, a second bedroom, and a second, smaller bath. In contrast to the outer walls built with wood, all interior walls were constructed with drywall, or gypsum fiber boards, which were additionally insulated with wool. Natural stone floors were installed in the kitchen, bath, and foyer. Exquisite walnut parquet was installed in all the other rooms.

← Due to heavy local rainfall, the property's soil is often very wet. Moreover, during sudden, heavy rainfalls there is a threat of brief periods of flooding. As a result, the building has been erected on stilts, so the water can easily drain away under the house.

Straw Insulation in the Attic, Geothermal and Solar Heat

The roof truss was constructed with open rafters. Straw was chosen as a simple insulation option. Compressed straw bales measuring 14" [35 cm] in width were installed two by two to fill gaps in the roof area. With regard to energy efficiency, 14" [35 cm] of straw bale insulation is equivalent to 10" [25 cm] of heavy wood fiber insulation, but with one big difference: insulating this home's entire roof with straw only cost $490 [350 Euros] (at an exchange rate of 1 Euro to $1.4). Because of a special, fire-resistant protective covering, the straw bales do not pose a fire hazard and, in their compressed and installed state, they do not burn easily. The heating needs of the home are met using a two-pronged strategy. The geothermal pump that is connected to a 1,722 square foot [160 sq. m] collector system installed below the ground frost line in the home's own garden supplies most of the heat. This feeds the low-energy radiant floor heating and provides warm water. In addition, a 43 ft 2 [4 m2] solar heat system on the roof heats water and supports the main heating system. Both systems are connected to a 79 gallon [300 liter] gray water tank and both function in a fully automatic and co-ordinated manner. Furthermore, a wood stove provides heat for both the lower and upper levels of the house. An attached 322 ft2 [30 m2] extension houses a workshop and the mechanical room. ●

N ➲ SITE PLAN

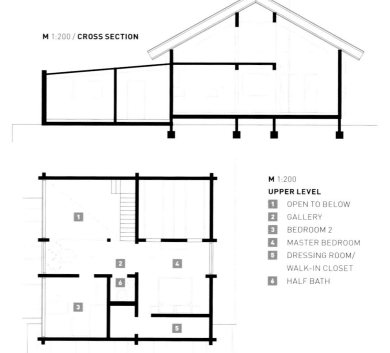

M 1:200 / **CROSS SECTION**

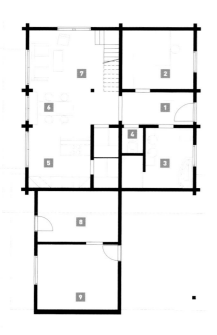

M 1:200
LOWER LEVEL

1	ENTRY
2	WORK
3	BATH
4	HALF BATH
5	KITCHEN
6	DINING
7	LIVING
8	STORAGE
9	GARAGE

M 1:200
UPPER LEVEL

1	OPEN TO BELOW
2	GALLERY
3	BEDROOM 2
4	MASTER BEDROOM
5	DRESSING ROOM/ WALK-IN CLOSET
6	HALF BATH

ℹ A total of approximately **1,695 ft³ [48 m³]** of wood volume was used in construction. This is equivalent to a carbon component in wood of **13.23 tons [12 metric tons]**, which is equivalent, in turn, to the storage of **48.5 tons [44 metric tons]** of carbon dioxide for 100 years.

MANUFACTURER	LOG BLOCKHAUS ING. THOMAS ZEILINGER GMBH
ARCHITECT	ING. THOMAS ZEILINGER
LOCATION	AUSTRIA, BURGENLAND
LOT SIZE	9,042 FT² [840 M²]
LIVING AREA	1,292 FT² [120 M²]
CONSTRUCTION COST	$252,000 [180,000 EURO]
	BASE OF CALCULATION: 1 EURO = $1.40 USD
COMPLETION	2008

↗ The light spruce wood, the rich grain of the walnut parquet floor, and the handmade log bed blend harmoniously..

→ Within a fairly small space, the design concept creates a cozy living room opening onto the south-facing terrace and easily accommodates the stairway to the upper level at no cost to comfort.

TUSCAN LOG HOUSE IN SPESSART

In the northernmost part of Spessart, a low, heavily wooded mountain range in Bavaria, Germany, nestles between the foothills of the Rhoen and Vogelsberg mountains. There stands a log house unlike any other.

The Spessart Nature Park [Naturpark Spessart], bordered by the Main River in the south and the German federal state of Hessen in the northwest, is the most wooded upland region in Germany. The rounded hilltops of this typical low mountain landscape, thickly covered with oak and beech forests, are only about 1,969 feet [600 meters] above sea level, which means that they are only slightly higher than the median total elevation.

Parapet and Sculptures Evoke Classical Antiquity
Just one look is enough to see that this home, with an exterior of traditionally hand-hewn, solid wood log beams, is a sublime masterpiece from top to bottom. Tuscany, the cradle of the Renaissance and European humanism, served as the inspiration for the home's design. The architectural and historical-cultural roots of this Austrian pine log house are evident in many of its features: the slightly sloped hip roof with overhanging parapet that functions as a rain gutter; the roofing of ridge and furrow pan tiles; floor-to-ceiling, vertically aligned windows with Mediterranean balusters to prevent falling; stone and iron sculptures reminiscent of ancient Rome and Greece; as well as an overall strict symmetry.

21st Century Winter Garden
A glass pyramid on the roof bathes the foyer in soft sunlight. To the left of the foyer in the two-story main house there is a spacious bedroom with its own bath, while to the right, there is an entry to the storage room, garage, and basement. The circular stairway in the foyer leads to the upper floor where there are three bedrooms in total with two bathrooms, one of which has a separate half-bath. Straight ahead through the foyer is the first-floor winter garden extension, which forms the center of the home's activities. Very much like a modern conservatory, the garden-side extension is a composite lumber and glass construction built with heat protective glazing. Outside, the upper sides of the extension's beams are capped with zinc plating to protect them from the elements. In the design of the extension, structural engineering and architectural aspiration have created a space that lives up to the grandeur of the main house.

Living in Light and Freedom
The free-flowing layout of the rooms follows the path of the sun. The first of two fully glassed-in bays contains the kitchen and the dining room facing southeast. This is followed to the south by the tasteful living room with its open fireplace. Finally, in the second bay facing west, there is a room for relaxation with a sauna and a ground-level whirlpool. The spacious living area with a total of 1,292 square feet [120 square meters] is supported by four steel posts. The walls on all sides were executed as full-length glass facades, so that the views of the home's park-like gardens and the valley beyond are unimpeded. At any time of the day and in all kinds of weather, the atmosphere in the house is buoyed by brightness and the close and visible presence of nature. Fittingly, the home enjoys peace and privacy on its lot of 48,438 square feet or 1.1 acre [4,500 square meters].

↗ If there were Roman log house gods, they would reign in a log house like this.

→ In this futuristic winter garden extension, the living room takes center stage, flanked on either side by a bay area.

46

← In this living area with antique flair,
the true powers of nature's elements are
combined with the creativeness of modern
wood construction craftsmanship.

↑ A dream of a
room with its own
balcony and bath.

↑ The custom kitchen is open to the dining and living room areas.

↓ The ground-level whirlpool in a side bay, with its unobstructed view of the Spessart, is a central element of the fitness and wellness area, which also has a sauna, a shower, and a rest and relaxation room.

↑ A grand entrance, indeed. This lordly, wooden double door raises both excitement and expectations. A defining design element for the entry area, the free-standing spiral staircase with a diameter of 8' [2.5 meters]. The stairs, sawn from 100-year-old wooden beams, were stacked and positioned on a central shaft.

Successful Symbiosis

All in all, this log house villa offers over 3,229 square feet [300 m2] of living space on two floors as well as a 2/3 basement level. The multi-layered, permeable, and moisture-regulating wall construction consists of a log wall made of 7" [18 cm] glued laminate timber, with 6" [15 cm] of cellulose insulation inside and finally a .78" [2 cm] layer of log wood paneling. Heat and hot water for the house, including the whirlpool, are provided exclusively by a fully automatic pellet stove, which feeds a low-energy radiant floor heating system on all floors. In addition, the complex is equipped with an adjustable heat, ventilation, and air conditioning (HVAC) system with heat recovery through an air-to-air heat pump. While the owner's love of history and log houses is evident in the main house, the winter garden extension openly reveals the spirit of twenty-first century architecture. ●

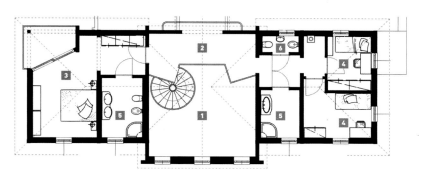

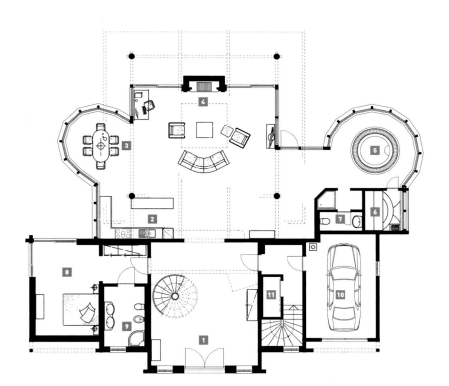

51

1 OPEN TO BELOW **4** CHILDREN'S BEDROOMS
2 GALLERY **5** BATHS
3 BEDROOM **6** HALF BATH

M 1:200 / **LOWER LEVEL**

1	ENTRY/FOYER	**7**	HALF BATH
2	KITCHEN	**8**	BEDROOM
3	DINING	**9**	BATH
4	LIVING	**10**	GARAGE
5	WHIRLPOOL	**11**	STORAGE
6	SAUNA		

MANUFACTURER	ELK-FERTIGHAUS AG
ARCHITECT	ANDJELKA WEINOLD, VIENNA
LOCATION	GERMANY, SPESSART
LOT SIZE	48,922 FT² OR 1.1 ACRES [4,545 M²]
LIVING AREA	3,229 FT² [300 M²]
CONSTRUCTION COST	$1,722,000 [1,230,000 EURO]
	BASE OF CALCULATION: 1 EURO = $1.40 USD
COMPLETION	2004

i A total of approximately **6,604 ft³ [187 m³]** of wood volume was used in construction. This is equivalent to a carbon component in wood of **51.53 tons [46.75 metric tons]**, which is equivalent, in turn, to the storage of **195.55 tons [177.4 metric tons]** of carbon dioxide for 100 years.

DREAM HOUSE FROM THE TREE OF LIFE

Wishes do come true not far from Germany's Fairy Tale Route. In a small rural community in the heart of Germany, a dream log house has become reality.

At the gate of the Spessart Nature Park [Naturpark Spessart], there stands a one-story Canadian-style log house at a height of 1,312 feet [400 meters]. The original idea of sustainable architecture with a layout that is as open as possible was developed and realized right next to 2,956 acres [1,200 hectares] of mixed forest, romantic villages, and historic palaces and castles. The desire for unrestricted views of the lovely landscape of rolling hills necessitated a structural compromise: the construction of a full basement because of the sloped lot. In only six months, a modern, one-story log house bungalow, including interiors, was constructed and finished. The hip roof with its gentle 18-degree slope adds a harmonious finishing touch to this home, pleasantly modest in look and feel. The mechanical room, a storage room, the work shop, the log house planning office, a second bath, as well as a cistern that collects and stores rainwater for use in the home are all located in the below-grade basement level made of Poroton blocks. The garage is also integrated into the basement level. Placed on top of the foundation, the log house provides 1,615 square feet [150 square meters] of living space on the ground level, or first floor, spread over an open-concept living-dining-kitchen area, a large master bedroom, two smaller bedrooms for the children, and a spacious family bathroom.

↖ Unlike the basement level made with Poroton blocks, the upper level was constructed with fine Canadian western red cedar wood.

← The low-sloped hip roof tops off the solid wood construction aptly.

Thuja Plicata—Western Red Cedar

The exposed roof structure with round jack, collar, and ridge beams is on average 20 to 24" [50 to 60 cm] thick. A total of 2,649 ft3 [75 cubic meters] of Canadian western red cedar with single trunks measuring up to 13.78" [35 cm] in diameter were used for construction. Thuja Plicata, which is also known as giant arborvitae—Latin for "tree of life"—belongs to the cypress family. Native to western North America, Thuja Plicata is called western red cedar because of the aromatic, spicy scent of its wood, but it does not belong to the cedar family. One of the tallest tree species in the world, it can grow to a height of about 200 feet [60 meters], and live longer than 1,200 years. Of particular interest are its high natural insulation properties, its durability, and its lasting resistance to fungal and insect infestation. In addition, western red cedar is sapless, resistant to weather and decay, and, therefore, very stable.

Inviting Arches

The living area features an open design concept in which the various rooms flow seamlessly into one another. Archways connect the living room, kitchen, and foyer harmoniously. The striking fireplace, with its wood stove, is not only the visual center of the space but also its energy center, with an integrated heat exchanger whose 15-kilowatt output provides heat and hot water for the home. Its design was conceived by the owner and log home planner himself, who not only personally embossed and laid the natural sandstone, but was also responsible for the elaborate copper and brass applications. A low-energy, radiant floor heating system is connected to the fireplace and works in the entire living tract, as well as in a large part of the basement. A screed floor built up to a thickness of 3.93" [10 cm] provides sufficient back-up storage. During peak load times, a gas boiler in the basement provides heat as needed.

A Love of Detail

A love of log house aesthetics is evident in the interior details as well. For example, in the bathroom, the sink sits atop a surprising but eye-catching red sandstone boulder. A ceiling was built over the bedroom areas in order to gain more space. Vertical openings through the ceiling lead directly from the children's rooms up into the area above the bedrooms and under the roof into a real "hide-out" with a large play area that the kids can reach by climbing a ladder right from their beds. The word "raccoon" comes from the Algonquin of North America and can be translated as "he who takes everything into his hands." How appropriate, then, that this log house, built by a man who has taken so very much into his own capable hands, is called "Racoon Hill"—even if the hill is in the middle of Hesse, Germany. ●

↑ Wide roof overhangs protect the log house from wind and weather.

↗ The feeling of wide-open space conveyed by the magnificent natural surroundings is reflected in the peace and comfort of the living room.

→ Protected by the massive ceiling and wall beams, the home owners can get a good night's sleep every night.

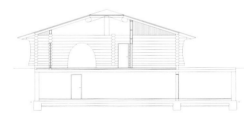

M 1:300 / **CROSS SECTION**

M 1:300
FIRST FLOOR

1 KITCHEN
2 LIVING
3 BATH
4 BEDROOMS (CHILDREN)
5 MASTER BEDROOM

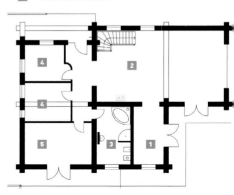

ℹ A total of approximately 2,649 ft³ [75 m³] of wood volume was used in construction. This is equivalent to a carbon component in wood of **20.6 tons [18.7 metric tons]**, which is equivalent, in turn, to the storage of **75.7 tons [68.7 metric tons]** of carbon dioxide for 100 years.

MANUFACTURER	DAS HOLZHAUS OLIVER SCHATTAT GMBH
ARCHITECT	FRANK BÜRGEL
LOCATION	GERMANY, SPESSART
LOT SIZE	10,850 FT² [1,008 M²]
LIVING AREA	1,615 FT² [150 M²]
CONSTRUCTION COSTS	$490,000 [350,000 EURO]
	BASE OF CALCULATION: 1 EURO = $1.40 USD
COMPLETION	2001

57

↓ The self-contained log house in the Spessart Nature Park [Naturpark Spessart] delights family, friends, and neighbors alike.

LOG HOUSE BUNGALOW ON THE GEEST RIDGE

Germany's Wingst, a small range of wooded hills where the Elbe River flows into the North Sea, is the home of a Canadian-style log house dream come true.

Northwest of the Hanseatic city, Hamburg, in the district of Cuxhaven, there is a landscape of unbroken peace and tranquility, the Wingst. Flat marshes and moors rising just above sea level surround the Geest ridge, a coastal heath land formed by the sandy deposits left by the moraines of the Ice Age. Nature alone rules here, peace and relaxation are the order of the day.

Diamond Notch

Following their natural preferences, the owners searched for and found the perfect location for their natural, hand-crafted log house. The house was planned thoroughly in advance and in close cooperation with the log house builder and the master carpenter, who together with the owners selected and winter felled the Douglas firs from the nearby forest that were used for construction. With an average diameter of approximately 14" [35 cm], the ten trunks form a structure of long-lasting strength. A recreation or guest house was built next to the main house on a building lot of over 23,142 square feet or .53 acre [2,150 square meters]. This handsome family complex is completed by a two-car garage, whose door was hand-crafted from weatherproof larch wood. The saddle notches, several less than 45 degrees, were executed as diamond notches, which have two rather than one saddle on the underside so that the upper and lower saddle cuts form the shape of a diamond. These double saddle notches make the house as tight as possible and able to withstand even the most unpredictable weather for the long run. For the roof construction, scissor trusses were built, which allow for the highest vaulted ceilings possible.

Custom-made One of a Kind

The handcrafted log house bungalow offers a total of 3,229 square feet [300 square meters] of living space. An elegant round archway-like entrance door sets the stage. The custom kitchen, an example of practical functionality, flows seamlessly into the central living room area. Quality 1.1" [28 mm] thick, wide oak plank flooring underscores the home's upscale character. The centrally located main living area forms an axis from which a side wing extends to the northeast. This side wing houses the home office in a semi-circular bay, as well as an expansive spa-like bathroom and the master bedroom. In the northwest section of the house are the guest room with its own small bathroom and the home's utility, or mechanical, room.

Open Living Area

A spacious living room—over 1,184 square feet [110 square meters] with 13-foot [4-meter] high ceilings—forms the heart of the entire residence. The room enjoys unobstructed views of the garden through wide glass doors that lead directly to the outdoor terrace. In the middle of the central living room stands a huge soapstone fireplace, whose bold style emphasizes the strong character of the natural log home. The Finnish natural fireplace is designed in such a way that it only needs to be heated once a day for about two hours to give off heat for the entire day because of its immense storage capacity.

→ The inviting entrance is flanked on one side by the semi-circular office bay and on the other by the two-car garage made of larch wood.

↘ Following pages: The handcrafted log complex built with local Douglas firs proves once again how beautiful solid wood construction can be.

← The spacious combination living area is heated by the Finnish soapstone wood stove, whose weight of over 2.2 tons [2 metric tons] leaves no room for doubt about its heating capacity.

← Roman bath culture combined with Canadian log house skill: the generously proportioned bath is illuminated in style with direct and indirect lighting.

Classical Bath Culture

The so-called tepidarium, with its roots in the ancient bath culture of the Romans, is a room for regeneration, preventative care, and healing. Hearkening back to the Roman tradition, the luxuriously tiled and generously proportioned bathroom uses the conductivity and the storage capacity of the heated tiles to keep the room evenly warm with natural radiant heat. The air is relatively dry and the temperature hovers at a mild 100 to 104 degrees Fahrenheit [38 to 40 degrees Celsius]. In this way, the immune system is strengthened without putting a strain on the body's circulatory system. Warmth and moisture stimulate circulation, clean out pores and lungs, loosen up muscles, and speed up metabolism—in conjunction with the moisture-regulating, solid wood log wall—a room for optimal rest and relaxation.

MANUFACTURER	HOLZBAU ANDREAS VOLLMERS
ARCHITECT	INGENIEURBÜRO FÜR BAUWESEN POSSE & GÖTZE
LOCATION	GERMANY, LOWER SAXONY
LOT SIZE	22,981 FT² OR .53 ACRES [2,135 M²]
LIVING AREA	3,229 FT² [300 M²]
CONSTRUCTION COST	$840,000 [600,000 EURO]
	BASE OF CALCULATION: 1 EURO = $1.40 USD
COMPLETION	2006

← The soapstone radiator mounted in forked Douglas fir branches separates the living room from the entrance area and is a real one-of-a-kind design element.

M 1:300
GROUND LEVEL

1 LIVING
2 DINING
3 KITCHEN
4 OFFICE
5 BATH
6 BEDROOM
7 GUEST
8 UTILITY

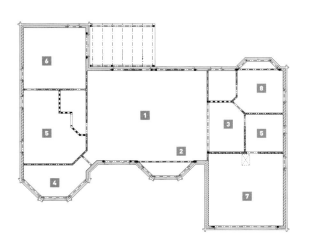

N ⬤ **SITE PLAN**

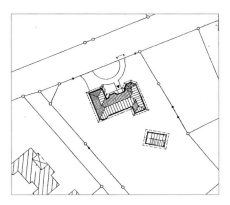

ⓘ A total of approximately **3,885 ft³ [110 m³]** of wood volume was used in construction. This is equivalent to a carbon component in wood of **30.3 tons [27.5 metric tons]**, which is equivalent, in turn, to the storage of **110.2 tons [100 metric tons]** of carbon dioxide for 100 years.

M 1:300 / **CROSS SECTIONS**

LOG HOUSE AMONG THE STONY PEAKS

The Mythen, a two-peaked mountain massif, is located in central Switzerland in the Schwyzer Voralpen, or the foothills of the Alps, in the canton of Schwyz. A Finnish log house brings contemporary log house style to this historic spot while reviving local home building tradition.

In the municipality of Alpthal, agriculture, forestry, and alpine farming are not merely cultural and historical achievements of a far-distant past. While the service sector dominates today's labor market throughout Europe, about half of the 540 residents of this Swiss municipality still make their living in the primary sector using skills attained thousands of years ago. This kind of historical persistence is as unique as the emblem of the Canton of Schwyz—the double peaks called the big and little Mythen.

Quality Wood Construction at a Height of 3,609 Feet [1,100 Meters]

The northern foot of the Mythen mountains is now the home of a solid wood house from the far northern reaches of Europe. The magnificent sloped site at the foot of the majestic twin peaks, watching over the valley like pyramids of stone, is complemented by the discerning architectural design and execution of the Finnish log house. The home nestles discreetly against the slope of the Alpthal meadows and fits in seamlessly in the village scene. The log house has a full basement and provides the owner's family of six, as well as their horse, dog, and cat, 3,229 square feet [300 square meters] of ample living space on the home's other stories. The multi-layered wall construction consists of a 7.87" [20-cm thick] laminated spruce log with a D profile, covered on the inside by a 3.94" [10-cm] thick layer of insulation, which in turn is finished by round log paneling of the same thickness.

Deep Black Elegance

Wide open living areas are interspersed with private, personal retreats and cheerful playrooms. Curved lines set an elegant counterpoint to the visible structural details of precise, linear carpentry. Jet-black "Nero Assoluto" gabbro, an intrusive (found below the surface), igneous rock, similar to volcanic basalt, was used for the gleaming, elegant floors. The polished surface of the tiles is very resilient, both chemically and physically, and does not dirty or scratch easily—perfect for a household with four children.

Concerted Living Space

The living room, with its glass walls under the gable, offers an open view of the roof construction at a lofty height of 26 feet [8 meters] and makes the rosewood grand piano sound as if it were in a concert hall. The open-concept design seamlessly incorporates the dining area and the tasteful, white, built-in kitchen. The first floor also provides ample space for a hobby room, a TV room, and a home office. On the second floor, there are four children's bedrooms, the master bedroom with a separate dressing area, and two full baths. The solid wood log house ties into age-old traditions dating back to the sixteenth and seventeenth centuries, when the export and processing of wood was of particular importance to the village. Now a gorgeous piece of woodwork has come home.

← The ancient and lofty peaks of the Mythen mountain watch over the Finnish log house.

← Window with a view: From the bedroom, the builders enjoy an impressive view of the mountain range in central Switzerland.

→ The open first lounge offers the ideal soundscape for the rosewood grand piano.

← The kitchen and dining area blend seamlessly. The polished surface of the stone tile floor is functional and stylish.

→ Having a permanent holiday in the clear mountain air: this healthy living log house includes a private pool, heated from the emissions-free geothermal system.

↑ The room divider serves as a book case in the living room and a garderobe in the entrance area.

↑ All of the wood work, window frames, doors, as well as the solid wood stairs were built to order and installed with painstaking precision.

N ◑ SITE PLAN

MANUFACTURER	POLAR LIFE HAUS—HONKATALOT
ARCHITECT	ABB ARCHITEKTUR BERATUNG BAUMELER
LOCATION	SWITZERLAND, CANTON OF SCHWYZ
LOT SIZE	14,402 FT² OR .33 ACRE [1,338 M²]
LIVING AREA	3,229 FT² [300 M²]
CONSTRUCTION COST	$1,776,600 [1,269,000 EURO]
	BASE OF CALCULATION: 1 EURO = $1.40 USD
CONSTRUCTION YEAR	2009

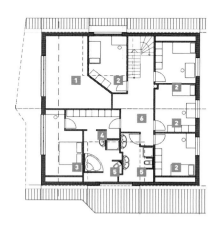

M 1:300 / **BASEMENT**

1 GARAGE
2 STORAGE
3 WASH ROOM
4 WINE CELLAR
5 MECHANICAL

M 1:300 / **FIRST FLOOR**

1 ENTRY
2 KITCHEN
3 DINING
4 LIVING
5 GUEST
6 OFFICE
7 HALF BATH
8 HOBBY ROOM

M 1:300 / **SECOND FLOOR**

1 OPEN TO BELOW
2 CHILDREN'S BEDROOMS
3 MASTER BEDROOM
4 DRESSING ROOM
5 BATH
6 GALLERY

Exceeding Requirements

The Swiss energy guidelines for low-energy houses, the so-called "Minergy Standards" were not only fulfilled but exceeded. The prescribed annual maximum of 42 kilowatt hours of fossil energy consumption per square meter over the gross area per floor was met effortlessly. A geothermal heat pump provides the entire house with heat and hot water year-round without producing any emissions. Because of its huge heating surface, the low-energy radiant floor heating system only needs a low flow temperature of about 95 degrees Fahrenheit [35 degrees Celsius]. As a result, the geothermal heat that feeds this system can also heat the swimming pool. •

i A total of approximately **8,228 ft³ [233 m³]** of wood volume was used in construction. This is equivalent to a carbon component in wood of **64.15 tons [58.2 metric tons]**, which is equivalent, in turn, to the storage of **235 tons [213.6 metric tons]** of carbon dioxide for 100 years.

↓ The spruce log house, whose gabled side looks onto the tranquil Alpthal, rests on a stone foundation.

↓ With its well-planned energy concept, the northern spruce house exceeds the Swiss energy guidelines for low-energy houses.

CASA BLANCA IN APULIA

In the extreme southeast of the Italian Adriatic region stands a South Tyrolean log house with modern accents and historical ties.

In Apulia, or Puglia, on the heel of the "Italian boot," where the Adriatic Sea meets the Ionian Sea on the Strait of Otranto, an exceptional log house basks in the light of the Hellenic sun. Although the basic idea for the complex and its detailed execution can be seen as a model for such construction, the home is the unique and individual creation of the architect and home owner himself, who lives in the stylish residence.

Flat-roof Bungalow

Gently nestled on the coastal plain among almond trees, wine gardens, and olive groves, this log house, built of solid wood on the interior as well as the exterior, fits into its ancient surroundings. The clean lines and well-conceived construction lend the flat-roof bungalow a refreshing functionality. The one-story log house made of solid spruce has a basic rectangular layout and houses three apartments in its 3,767 square feet [350 square meters]. The almost level roof was covered with very flat concrete roof tiles, which are well-suited for structures with slight slopes. A meticulously constructed dry-stone wall defines boundaries and completes the coherent overall concept.

Greek Legacy

Apulia underwent many changes throughout its history. It once belonged to the Roman Empire, experienced various great migrations, and was for a long time the seat of Greek colonies. The Greek influence, in particular, is still evident today, for example, in the blinding white of Apulia's architecture, which suits its climate so well. With these ancient origins in mind, the architect selected a South Tyrolean log house manufacturer steeped in tradition, who offered a log wall system named "Casa Blanca" (white house) that

was capable of effectively combating both Apulia's summer heat and the wet Mediterranean winters. The multi-layered, permeably insulated, wall and roof construction combines the comfortable log house atmosphere with the elegance of a white façade: a healthy natural climate on the inside; light-reflecting radiance on the outside.

Well-planned Design

The log home's interiors feature sliding doors made of frosted glass, which create a light and airy atmosphere while saving space. The roughly 10' [3-meter] high ceiling construction extends the architect's design concept upward, where narrow skylights keep the rooms bright, while keeping out excessive heat. Wood paneling with open support and roof beams on one side and white paint on walls and spaces between the rafters on the other side create a balanced contrast. Beams and rafters were left exposed on purpose to underscore the log house character of the structure. The roof heating system with its integrated solar equipment and heat pump generates pleasant radiant heat while saving space and energy, since the large heating surface allows the system to function at a lower flow temperature. Allergy sufferers can also breathe easy: in this type of log house, much less dust gets stirred up. ●

→ A logical consequence of modern architecture: solid wood construction in Bauhaus style.

72

← Bright, friendly, and functional: narrow hallways lead directly to all the rooms of this one-story log house.

→ Festive evening mood in Mezzogiorno, Italy's southern region, which forms its "boot." The white and brown accents of this wooden house create a lovely backdrop for the ancient olive trees.

→ On the street side as well, the home's look is characterized by its orderly restraint and clean edges.

The Ancient and the Modern

A continuous, partially sheltered, garden-side veranda with horizontally installed wood paneling was integrated into the structural shell. Full-height veranda windows built into the structure not only ensure that there is always enough light inside, but also that the veranda will have enough shade right into the afternoon hours. With this project, the traditional log house manufacturer from South Tyrol has once again created an impressive and carefully planned log home with its modular elements. ●

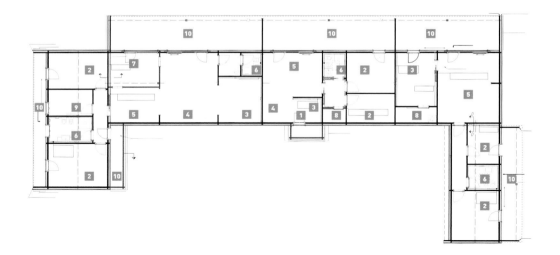

M 1:300

GROUND LEVEL N ⊙

1	ENTRY
2	BEDROOM
3	KITCHEN
4	DINING
5	LIVING
6	BATH
7	OFFICE
8	STORAGE
9	WALK-IN CLOSET
10	TERRACE

MANUFACTURER	RUBNER HAUS AG
ARCHITECT	FRANCESCO LONGANO
LOCATION	ITALY, APULIA
LOT SIZE	NOT SPECIFIED
LIVING AREA	3,767 FT² [350 M²]
CONSTRUCTION COSTS	NOT SPECIFIED
COMPLETION	2008

↗ Partition walls are passé. In this open concept design, the living spaces flow into one another, but still retain their own contours.

→ The home's clean lines are defined by contemporary design and subtle variation in material and color selection.

ℹ A total of approximately **6,357 ft³ [180m³]** of wood volume was used in construction. This is equivalent to a carbon component in wood of **49.6 tons [45 metric tons]**, which is equivalent, in turn, to the storage of **181.8 tons [165 metric tons]** of carbon dioxide for 100 years.

RESIDENTIAL, COMMERCIAL, AND MODEL LOG HOUSE

On the northern shore of Lake Zurich, in the southeastern part of the Swiss canton of Zurich, this multifunctional log house is located right next to a building center for log house construction.

A natural custom log house, with an expansive 3,013 square feet [280 square meters] of living space on two floors, rests on a brick foundation. Constructed with massive trunk logs measuring 13.7" to 21.6" [35 to 55 cm] in diameter, this house was built to last. In total, a considerable 250 cubic meters of silver fir was felled in the winter by the builder himself, peeled, or barked, using high pressure water, and used for construction. The wood comes from sustainable-growth forests in the region and was examined and selected in conjunction with the local foresters. The house mechanical room, various storage rooms, and a workshop are located in the basement.

Full Silver Fir Construction

The wood from the silver fir, also known as the European fir, is relatively light in color and elastic. It dries quickly, shrinks very little, and as a result does not have many settling problems. In addition, it is resin-free and has an even structure. Moreover, compared to other wood varieties, silver fir wood keeps its natural color for a long time, even when subjected to light, darkening only a little. It is similar to spruce in regard to its flexibility and ability to withstand pressure, which make it a suitable wood for construction. In addition, it can easily be combined with other building materials like glass, steel, or stone, offering the modern log house construction diverse possibilities for variation.

Wool Insulation

In contrast to the solid, peeled log exterior walls, the interior walls were all, save one, built with lightweight stud construction. Local wool was installed as insulation between the individual wood studs in addition to the usual compressed, expanding foam insulation tape. On the outside, wide roof overhangs of up to 8.2 feet [2.5 meters] protect the natural log structure from wind and weather. On the home's western side, knobby trunk log posts support a projecting roof. As a result, evenings can be enjoyed in the outdoor sitting area located there, regardless of the weather.

Saddle Notch

The home's unusual pentagonal floor plan expands the design possibilities in regard to laying out and dimensioning space. The beams that form the fifth corner of the house by meeting at a 160 degree angle were joined together with saddle notches. This type of notch originally comes from Canada and is one of the most reliable notches when it comes to weatherproofing and elimination of thermal leaks. In saddle notching, U-shaped notches, or grooves in the shape of a saddle, are cut into the tops and bottoms of logs. Logs are then stacked so that the downturned notch of the upper log rests in the groove of the up-turned notch of the bottom log, forming a solidly interlocked structure. In this way, the logs stay in place perfectly without cracking or splitting, even as the wall settles.

← The house's fifth corner with its saddle notches opens up new options for interior design and layout in this residential and office log construction.

→ Next page: Enjoy the cozy but elegant atmosphere under the glassed-in, open gallery gable as the flames flicker in the fireplace whose chimney pipe seems to hang free-floating above.

MANUFACTURER	BLOCKHAUSBAU PORRENGA GMBH
ARCHITECT	MAX WINTSCH
LOCATION	SWITZERLAND, CANTON OF ZURICH
LOT SIZE	26,910 FT² [2,500 M²]
LIVING AREA	3,014 FT² [280 M²]
CONSTRUCTION COST	$789,600 [564,000 EURO]
	BASE OF CALCULATION: 1 EURO = $1.40 USD
COMPLETION	2005

↓ The exposed purlins and rafters of the roof construction over the open gallery level.

↑ Dark-gray, seamless, and low-maintenance anhydrite flooring was installed on the first level. This type of flooring is completely customizable thanks to the many different finishing options it offers—it can be custom-colored and finished, sanded, oiled, or sealed to create one-of-a-kind floors for every home.

Comfortable Log Heating

An electronically controlled log burning, or biomass, heating system with a 925 gallon [3,500-liter] buffer storage tank feeds the low-energy radiant floor heating system on all floors and provides hot water. The boiler can accommodate very large logs of up to 3.28 feet [one meter] in length, which means that, even in winter, the system only needs to be fed at conveniently long intervals—once every two days or so. All together, approximately 3.31 cords of wood [equivalent to 12 steres of wood, or cubic meters of piled wood], is used annually for every 3,937 cubic feet [1,200 cubic meters] of interior space (1 cubic meter = 1 stere = metric unit of volume used for measuring wood including empty space between wood pieces). This log house, which is used as a residence, a commercial office, and a model home, leaves nothing to be desired because it simply has it all—quality of life with all the modern amenities, well-planned functionality, as well as the sustainability and durability of twenty-first century wood architecture. •

ℹ️ A total of approximately **8,829 ft³ [250 m³]** of wood volume was used in construction. This is equivalent to a carbon component in wood of **68.89 tons [62.5 metric tons]**, which is equivalent, in turn, to the storage of **252.4 tons [229 metric tons]** of carbon dioxide for 100 years.

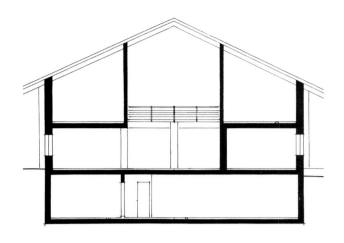

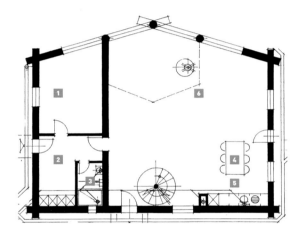

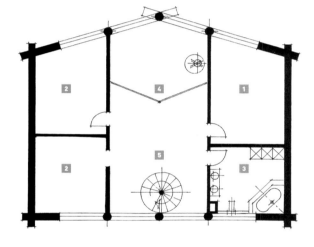

M 1:200 / **LOWER LEVEL**

1	WORK/OFFICE	4	DINING
2	STORAGE	5	KITCHEN
3	BATH/HALF-BATH	6	LIVING

M 1:200 / **UPPER LEVEL**

1	BEDROOM—CHILD	4	OPEN TO BELOW
2	MASTER BEDROOM	5	GALLERY
3	BATH		

→ Soak in the natural beauty of the massive silver fir trunk logs.

MASTERPIECE IN ICHTERBERG

A master carpenter from Germany's Eifel region builds with solid Douglas fir and adds stylish contrasting elements.

This log house was built on a wooded slope at an elevation of about 1,476 feet [450 meters] in a village in Germany's western Eifel region. The Douglas fir used for construction came from the region and is considered to be one of the harder softwoods. By nature, this species is very durable and resistant to fungal growth. It is also relatively light in weight and is, for all these reasons, particularly well-suited for use in construction. The side wing of the house was built parallel to the slope and has only one story, while the main wing of the house faces the valley and has one and a half stories. The center of the house is an expansive living area with soaring 16' 5" [5-meter] high ceilings, an open gable roof with exposed beams, and full glass walls that offer an unobstructed view of the lovely landscape of low mountains. A double-sided, exposed wall of limestone functions as a spectacular room divider between the dining and the living room areas and faces a matching limestone wall in the living room, which elegantly frames that room's wood stove near an outer wall.

A Terrace of First-Class Durability

Stone comes into play as a design element once again in the exterior composition: all around the log house a type of limestone gravel, which is common to the region, was used for drainage and for stabilizing and reinforcing the slope embankments. One of the home's most eye-catching features is its extensive terrace, which is, for the most part, covered. It wraps around the house from the south to the southwest side and rests on strong concrete columns or piers. Pine planks that had been treated with acetic anhydride were laid over an area of a total of 966 square feet [90 square meters]. This wood keeps insects away and does not swell. As a result, it is more resistant and durable than tropical exotic hardwoods. The planks gleam like oak and the stainless steel railings complete the terrace design.

DIY Interior Design

As a qualified master carpenter, trained architect, and designer, the house owner did a lot of the interior work himself. The results are impressive: whether it's the Corian® solid surface illuminated kitchen unit, or the high-end maple doors, or the limed oak dining table and matching chairs—the owner designed and executed everything himself and with a painstaking love of detail. Throughout the 1,938 square feet [180 square meters] of living space, either real oak plank flooring from the Eifel region was installed or a slate-like dark stone flooring was used as a contrasting element. The roomy master bedroom features a walnut wood bed built by the homeowner himself. To the left of the bed's headboard, a doorway leads to the luxurious master bath. To the right is a walk-in closet with lots of space.

Refined, Not Rustic

The children's room is located directly under the gabled roof on the top floor. Its wide overhang protects the large, roof-top terrace, as well as the rest of the house, from driving rain year round. Another smaller guest bedroom, a second bath, and a house utility room are also located on this floor. From the beginning, the homeowners, along with the architect and the master carpenter, planned for a light, transparent, and modern design. The interior's white plaster walls, built by using lightweight construction techniques, stand in deliberate contrast to the sturdy Douglas fir logs on the home's exterior. This conceptual approach of deliberate contrasts can be seen again in the exterior paint choices. The Douglas fir logs were treated with a gray-blue water-based wood stain with a precisely defined pigment content. The subtle hue, which was also

↗ Built on a steep, wooded slope, this log house of Douglas fir shows modern solid wood architecture at its best.

→ A double carport, a utility room, a storage place for wood, and the air heat pump are all located on the slope side.

used on the triple-glazed wood windows, harmonizes well with the mixed beech and pine tree forest that surrounds the log home.

Sustainable Forestry and Moon-Phase, Winter-Harvested Wood

The moisture-regulating, multi-layered wall construction is 14.2 inches [36 centimeters] thick. It consists of a 6.3″ [16-cm] thick round log layer, a 4.7″ [12-cm] thick layer of insulation, space for plumbing and utility connections, as well as the final layer of plasterboard for the interior plaster.

An air heat pump works almost soundlessly to serve the low-energy, radiant floor heating system installed on both stories and to provide hot water. A total of 8,530 feet [2,600 running meters] of air-dried Douglas fir wood were used for construction and immediately reforested, because the log house builders of the Eifel region take care of the natural source of their craft with true conviction. They cooperate with the local forestry agencies in a certified model that guarantees that more Douglas firs will be planted in the Eifel forests in the coming year than are felled in the previous winter in the phase of the new moon. ●

ℹ A total of approximately **4,096 ft³ [116 m³]** of wood volume was used in construction. This is equivalent to a carbon component in wood of **31.97 tons [29 metric tons],** which is equivalent, in turn, to the storage of **117 tons [106 metric tons]** of carbon dioxide for 100 years.

MANUFACTURER	FLOSS ZIMMEREI UND BLOCKHAUSBAU GMBH
ARCHITECT	PETER FLOSS
LOCATION	GERMANY, EIFEL
LOT SIZE	21,528 FT² OR .49 ACRE [2,000 M²]
LIVING AREA	1,938 FT² [180 M²]
CONSTRUCTION COST	NOT SPECIFIED
COMPLETION	2010

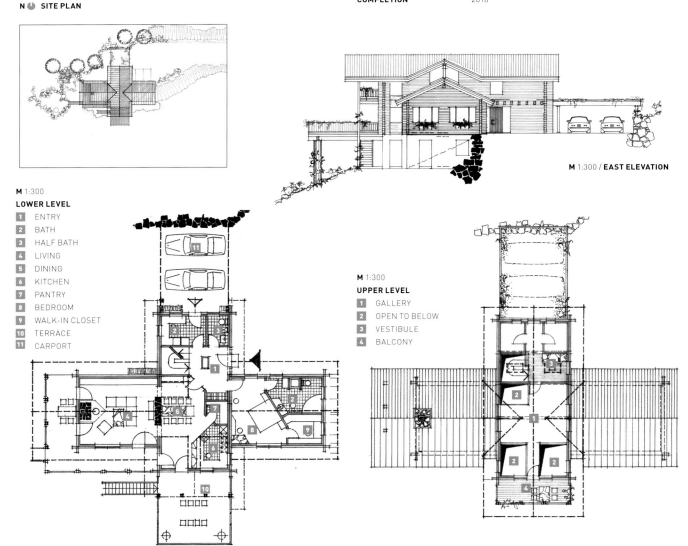

N ⊙ **SITE PLAN**

M 1:300 / **EAST ELEVATION**

M 1:300
LOWER LEVEL
1 ENTRY
2 BATH
3 HALF BATH
4 LIVING
5 DINING
6 KITCHEN
7 PANTRY
8 BEDROOM
9 WALK-IN CLOSET
10 TERRACE
11 CARPORT

M 1:300
UPPER LEVEL
1 GALLERY
2 OPEN TO BELOW
3 VESTIBULE
4 BALCONY

↑ An interior design coup, the illuminated Corian kitchen unit.

↑ In the living room, the building materials of wood, natural stone, and glass combine to form one clear design statement about true quality of life.

↓ Perfect in every detail, the southwestern wrap-around terrace made with a new type of extremely weatherproof wood planking.

WITH TRADITION INTO THE MODERN

A log house in northern Berchtesgaden Land in Bavaria, Germany, succeeds in creating a symbiosis between the renewable resource of wood and the renewable energy of the sun.

In the heart of the historical Rupertiwinkel area of Bavaria, right on the border to Salzburg, Austria, the city of Mozart, a spruce log house delights both lovers of the traditional and those who prefer the modern. With its ancient salt trade routes and its agricultural roots, this landscape, typical for the foothills of the Alps and shaped by the Salzach and Saalach rivers, has a long and important cultural history. Located at about 1,476 feet [450 meters] above sea level, this multi-layered log construction takes into account the area's historical and cultural heritage.

Solid Through and Through

Built on a gently sloping lot, the log house has a traditionally rectangular layout, intersected only by an addition. Like the house, this addition is also of solid wood log construction, which functions as a two-car garage with a workroom below. The wood used for construction comes from local mountain forests growing at a height of 2,625 feet [800 meters] above mean sea level. It was felled in the winter and was kiln-dried to a residual moisture content of approximately 14 percent before it was used for construction. A fully automatic, 10 kW wood chip system feeds the low-energy radiant floor heating that was installed on all levels, as well as the 317 gallon [1,200 liter] buffer storage tank for hot water.

↖ Breathe easy in this log house built with local spruce from sustainable forestry and a solar-powered energy supply.

← Comfort and convenience as far as the eye can see: two balconies, a wrap-around terrace, a two-car garage, and a central gabled roof—log house construction at its best.

Exemplary Energy Concept

The 1,307 cubic feet [37 cubic meter] wood chip storage bin located in the basement is filled automatically through a chute in the back of the house. In the living room, a custom-crafted traditional tiled masonry heater with integrated water technology and an 8 kW capacity is an additional source of comfortable radiant heat. The heater is connected to an old-fashioned oven like the ones in grandmother's time, when cooking, roasting, and baking were done directly on the hearth. Finally, a dual solar energy combination was attached to the roof: a 431-square-foot [40 square meter] photovoltaic system for producing electricity and a 215-square-foot [20 square meter] solar thermal energy system for heating water outside of the heating season. To provide for the energy needs of the log house alone, such a high-performance wood chip heating system would not have been necessary. However, the owner plans to construct outbuildings and a swimming pool in the future and the present system will be more than able to meet future energy needs.

Setting the Tone with Wood

The combination of tried and true carpentry traditions and new discoveries from research and development speaks loud and clear. One telling example: the traditionally alpine "Tiroler Schloss" or Tyrolean Lock notch style, which is known in the English-speaking world as the dovetail notch, combined with a multi-layered wall construction: an inner 1.57" [4 cm] thick spruce wood block frame is followed by a 1.18" [3-cm] ventilated cavity—an empty layer of air as insulation, topped by a 3.93" [10-cm] thick wood fiber board insulation, which, in turn, is covered by a 4.72" [12-cm] thick spruce log wall. This air-permeable but tightly insulating wall construction does not require artificial vapor barriers or foil insulation—wood alone does the job. The living room with its open gallery area, the dining room, and the kitchen are all located on the spacious, open-concept lower level. Also on this level are two of-

→ Friendly, bright, and spacious: the bathroom with sauna fulfills all of the homeowner's bath and relaxation wishes.

fices or work rooms, the panty, and a guest powder room. The high knee wall on the upper floor makes it possible to use the entire level to accommodate four bedrooms. The central family bathroom is generously proportioned and features a log wall sauna and a steam shower as well.

The Right Overall Balance

Modern interior design for galleries: without losing its bright transparency, the airy gallery was turned into usable space by the installation of a bridge made of glass that can be walked on. Three balconies on the second floor as well as a wrap-around terrace-like porch on the first floor offer panoramic views of the foothills of the Alps. The combination of renewable resources and renewable energy, not only in the home's construction, but also in the way its energy needs are met, sets new benchmarks for contemporary architecture in attaining an ecological balance. ●

↓ Next to the traditional tiled masonry heater with its integrated oven, there is room for a snack at the bar-height counter or for family meals with all the fixings at the dining table.

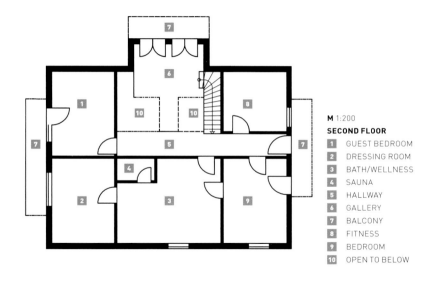

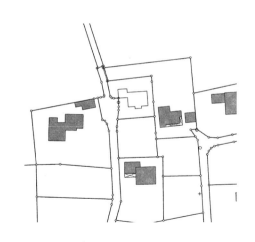

89

M 1:200
SECOND FLOOR
1 GUEST BEDROOM
2 DRESSING ROOM
3 BATH/WELLNESS
4 SAUNA
5 HALLWAY
6 GALLERY
7 BALCONY
8 FITNESS
9 BEDROOM
10 OPEN TO BELOW

M 1:200
FIRST FLOOR
1 ENTRANCE
2 KITCHEN
3 LIVING
4 PANTRY
5 UTILITY/MECHANICAL
6 HALF BATH
7 WORK/OFFICE
8 DINING
9 GARAGE
10 TERRACE

M 1:200 / **CROSS SECTION**

ℹ️ A total of approximately **4,944 ft³ [140 m³]** of wood volume was used in construction. This is equivalent to a carbon component in wood of 38.5 tons **[35 metric tons]**, which is equivalent, in turn, to the storage of **141 tons [128 metric tons]** of carbon dioxide for 100 years.

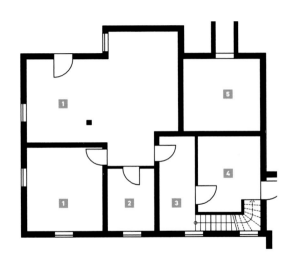

M 1:200
BASEMENT LEVEL
1 UNFINISHED BASEMENT
2 BATH
3 HALLWAY
4 HEATING
5 WOOD CHIP STORAGE BIN

MANUFACTURER + ARCHITECT	CHIEMGAUER HOLZHAUS
LOCATION	GERMANY, BAVARIA
LOT SIZE	7718 FT² [717 M²]
LIVING AREA	2,691 FT² [250 M²]
CONSTRUCTION COST	$252,000 [180,000 EURO] [INSTALLATION SUPERVISION]
COMPLETION	2004

AT HOME IN NATURE

Finland is not only the "land of a thousand lakes" but also the land of log house construction.

North of Wiesbaden, the capital of the federal state of Hesse, Germany, in the Rhine Taunus Nature Park, there is a Finnish log house of lavish beauty in a village that lies a good 1,312 feet [400 meters] above sea level. On this southern flank of the Taunus mountain range extensive, mixed deciduous forests of maple, ash, larch, and above all beech, alternate with meadows, fields, and pastures.

One-layer, Round Log House Construction
Built on a gently sloping lot, this log house of one-and-a-half stories sits atop a gray-blue stone foundation. Its one-layer wall construction consists of 9" [23-cm] thick round logs from the heartwood of the polar pine. On the north side of the house there is a two-car garage, another log construction, built parallel to the street. On the east, south, and west sides there are three large gables with large windows that let lots of light and warmth stream inside. The large pine gridded windows set all around the walls and the French doors on the garden-side also let in sunshine.

Clean Forms and Lines
The striking lines of the 38-degree pitched roof are accentuated by natural slate tiles. A sheltered storage space for fire wood adjoins the large terrace that wraps around the house on its southwestern side. On the basement level, there are three bedrooms for the children on the home's walk-out front side. Across the hall from the sleeping quarters on the rear side of the basement level, which is below grade, there is a three-quarter bathroom, a room for the heating equipment, as well as another utility/mechani-

cal room, and a storage room. On the first floor, beside the entryway and its foyer, a three-quarter bathroom for guests and a small storage room adjoin the kitchen, which features a central breakfast island. Beyond the kitchen, an open-concept dining room is heated and completed by a craftsman-built, traditional tiled masonry heater, making this the perfect space for entertaining large groups.

Comfortable Corners and Cozy Nooks
The ceilings, with their exposed round log beams, are the model of timeless, traditional wood construction. In parts of the interior, light construction walls were built in juxtaposition to the solid log walls to provide a stylistically contrasting design element. On the upper level, in the bathroom as well as the work room, large dormers provide natural light through impressive, rectangular, exposed beam roof construction. The master bedroom and a comfortable studio room for reading or listening to music complete the upper level of this Finnish dream log house. Porcelain stoneware flooring was installed on the floors of the lower level, while country pine plank flooring was selected for the upper level.

Polar Pine—Resistant and Efficient
Scotch, or Scots, pine (Pinus sylvestris) is a species of the pine genus of the pine family (Pinaceae). North of about the 65th parallel, near the Arctic Circle, this type of pine becomes what is known as polar pine in northeastern Europe. Because of the long winters, the summer growing season is cut very short with the result that the polar pines grow extremely slowly. These special growth conditions can be clearly discerned in the very close and narrow tree ring formation of this type of pine. The wood of polar pine, as a result, possesses good dimensional stability with a relatively high density and a correspondingly high dead load. Moreover, the polar pine grows very straight and its wood has an even structure. The farther north the pine grows, the closer its tree rings, and the more solid and

← Nestled in a beautifully landscaped yard, this lovely log house constructed with high-quality polar pine wood is filled with light through its many windows

↑ In the upstairs bathroom, there is
eye-catching dormer construction with
exposed beams.

↑ With its exposed beams, the relatively small but cozy living room under the roof still feels open and spacious.

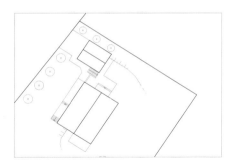

i A total of approximately **4,414 ft³ [125 m³]** of wood volume was used in construction. This is equivalent to a carbon component in wood of **34.4 tons [31.25 metric tons]**, which is equivalent, in turn, to the storage of **126.2 tons [114.5 metric tons]** of carbon dioxide for 100 years.

MANUFACTURER	HONKAREKENNE OYJ
ARCHITECT	ROLAND BOTT
LOCATION	GERMANY, TAUNUS
LOT SIZE	26,910 FT², OR .62 ACRES [2,500 M²]
LIVING AREA	3,391 FT² [315 M²]
CONSTRUCTION COST	$672,000 [480,000 EURO]
	BASE OF CALCULATION: 1 EURO = $1.40 USD
COMPLETION	2004

M 1:300 / **CROSS SECTION**

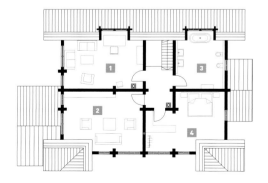

M 1:300
UPPER/ATTIC LOFT LEVEL
1. WORK/OFFICE
2. MUSIC/FAMILY ROOM
3. BATH
4. MASTER BEDROOM

M 1:300
BASEMENT LEVEL
1. BEDROOMS
2. BATH
3. HEATING EQUIPMENT
4. STORAGE
5. UTILITY/MECHANICAL

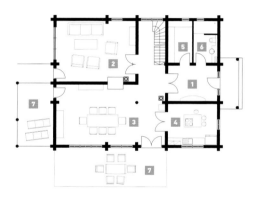

M 1:300
LOWER LEVEL
1. ENTRY
2. LIVING
3. DINING
4. KITCHEN
5. CLOSET
6. BATH
7. TERRACE

resistant its wood. It takes about 80 to 150 years before sustainably grown polar pine can be felled.

Its high resin content makes this wood very resistant to moisture. The resin also acts as an antibacterial and preservative agent. Furthermore, the heartwood of the polar pine contains a natural insecticide and fungicide, which is toxic to harmful fungal growths, bacteria, and insects, thereby providing the wood with lasting protection from decomposition. The natural insulating value of polar pine wood walls is many times greater than that of brick or concrete walls of the same thickness.

The home has a modular concept for meeting its energy requirements. Heat and hot water are provided by a modern, but traditional looking, masonry heater with a room boiler and a rated heating capacity of 14.9 kilowatts, which is centrally located in the large dining room. Connected to the heater is a 792.5 gallon [3,000 liter] combi-storage tank, including a solar heat exchanger, which feeds the low-energy radiant floor heating system on the first and second floors. Integrated into this overall energy design, a 172-square-foot [16-square meter] solar system with flat plate collectors mounted on the roof provides hot water in the summer and supports the heating system in the colder months.●

→ The blue-gray stones of this glowingly beautiful log house's foundation set a lovely contrast. The garage harmonizes with the two dormers.

→ The spacious dining room, with its views of the garden, is the center of family life.

THE ART OF POST-MODERN LOG HOUSE CONSTRUCTION

On Schliersee, a lake in Bavaria's Kalkalpen mountains in Germany, one manufacturer brings log house construction into the post-modern with a combination of masterly meticulousness and design clarity.

The overall design concept of this natural log house is evident in the exact symmetry of its floor plan, the precision craftsmanship of its details, and its harmonious transitions. The silver fir wood, with an average diameter of 16.5" [42 cm], used for construction, came from the over 3,281' [1,000 m] high mountains of the neighboring municipality of Jachenau. The region of Upper Bavaria is well-known for its densely wooded mountain slopes, which produce wood of the best quality through sustainable forestry. The home's lower level was constructed with round logs in classic fashion. In contrast, the first two log courses of the projecting upper level were built with flat-hewn logs. The resulting form, flattened on two sides, resembles the rough-hewn log of an almost squared-off beam. An upper level of timber frame construction was placed on top of this log base. The result was a three-part harmony in wood, as the three construction styles transitioned seamlessly into one another. Avoiding any rustic clumsiness in form, this solid wood construction blends diverse but harmonious components to form a unique, integrated look.

Larch Shingles
Classic saddle notches were used on the ground floor, while draft-proof, perfectly executed dovetail notches were chosen for the top floor. The outer walls of the upper level, which had been insulated with a 7" [18-cm] thick layer of soft wood fiber board, were clad with weather-resistant larch shingles, instead of the usual wood siding. This once again smoothed the rough edges of the log house look and added a lighter note to the striking façade. The scope of work performed by the log house manufacturer was quite comprehensive: from the design concept and planning, to the manufacturing and assembly on the manufacturer's factory building site, all the way to the construction of the framework, and the final assembly of all structural elements including the roof truss on the home's building site. The roof gutters—also made of larch wood—have specially forged brackets and an impressive length of 59 feet [18 meters]. Because of its flat valley location and a stream that runs through the building lot, the log house could not have a basement level.

Wood and Clay
The roof, which is also a log structure with exposed beams, was insulated with 7.1" [18 cm] of fiberboard. The local weather conditions can place great loads on the rooftops in this region, known as a "snow trap," so they were given much consideration when it came to determining the roof's dimensions. The roof, with a pitch of 22.5 degrees, has clay tiles and 6' 7" [2 m] wide overhangs that shelter the house structure. The post-modern design concept is continued consistently in the interior as well. Large sashless windows and smooth, flat walls that have been mudded with natural clay and white-washed provide a stylish contrast to the pervasive natural wood elements. Moreover, the natural materials, wood and clay, go especially well together. Both are permeable and help ensure a healthy indoor climate. Black tile flooring was installed throughout the entire log house. The selection of walnut cabinets gives the kitchen its strikingly clean lines. The bathroom makes an impact with its transparent openness, along with its combination bathtub and heated tile relaxation bed, with its ergonomically designed shape and heated surface.

↗ Atop the solid log lower level sits the upper level with its expansive glassed-in gable, built in the timber frame construction method.

→ In the modern kitchen with walnut cabinetry there is a wood stove and oven combination that can be used for cooking as well as heating.

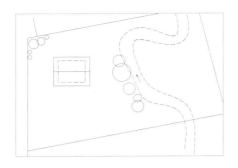

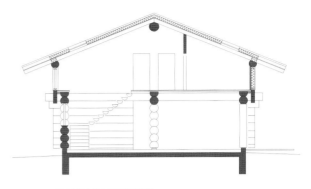

M 1:200 / **CROSS SECTION**

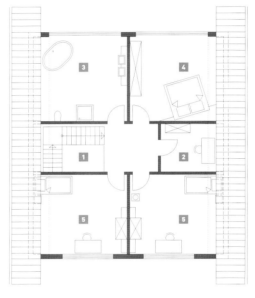

M 1:200
LOWER LEVEL

1 ENTRY/CLOSET
2 HALLWAY
3 BATH 3/4
4 GUEST BEDROOM
5 LIVING
6 DINING
7 KITCHEN
8 STORAGE

M 1:200
UPPER LEVEL

1 HALLWAY
2 OFFICE
3 BATH
4 MASTER BEDROOM
5 BEDROOM 2 / CHILD

i A total of approximately **6,357 ft³ [180 m³]** of wood volume was used in construction. This is equivalent to a carbon component in wood of **49.6 tons [45 metric tons]**, which is equivalent, in turn, to the storage of **181.8 tons [165 metric tons]** or of carbon dioxide for 100 years.

MANUFACTURER	ARTIFEX GMBH
ARCHITECT	CAROLA ULLMANN
LOCATION	GERMANY, BAVARIA
LOT SIZE	38,750 FT² OR .89 ACRES [3,600 M²]
LIVING AREA	2,099 FT² [195 M²]
CONSTRUCTION COST	$532,000 [380,000 EURO]
	BASE OF CALCULATION: 1 EURO = $1.40 USD
COMPLETION	2009

Spatial Conception on Equal Footing

This architecture of mixed styles places emphasis on both traditional and modern approaches with its design conception that reflects today's lifestyle. Horizontally and vertically flowing transitions ensure spatial freedom and openness without neglecting the need for private space. The home's energy needs are met by an emissions-free geothermal solution. Flat geothermal collectors laid in the garden feed the geothermal heat pump, which transfers the heat through the low-energy radiant floor heating system on both stories while it also provides hot water. The sleek, enameled kitchen range, which is heated with logs, is not only used to prepare delicious meals over an open flame but is also connected to the central heating system to supply additional heat to the home. ●

↑ The natural log house, expertly constructed with clean, simple lines.

→ The exquisite bathroom with its heated tile relaxation bed can be appreciated by all, not just log house fans.

→ The three-quarter bathroom on the lower level has direct access to the garden.

A REAL PIECE OF CANADA

A natural log house, planned with care and thought, rises up from the wide-open lowlands of northwestern Germany.

The dream of a life in the great outdoors came true for this family of four in their Canadian-style, traditional, hand-crafted log home. The wood, which came from the protected high forests of Germany's scenic Hunsruck region, was felled in winter in the lunar phase before the new moon. In total, over 3,937 feet [1,200 running meters] of Douglas fir wood, with an average diameter of 15.7" [40 cm], was used for construction. The house, built without a basement, offers over 4,306 ft2 [400 m2] of living space on two floors. The large pitched roof with its wide overhang of 8.2 feet [2.5 meters] provides the house with shelter from driving rains. The projecting, flying purlins underscore the pristine power of the solid wood construction. The log home has a mixed stone foundation built of stone blocks of different sizes, colors, and shapes, and its own stream that edges the home serenely as it provides drainage for the lot.

Four-Point Saddle Notch

Each and every log in this hand-crafted home was worked with axe, chainsaw, and chisel. Wool was inserted as insulation, or chinking, into the notches cut into each trunk. In addition to this, the manufacturer used other self-developed chinking and daubing techniques in the notches to insulate and seal. In order to avoid cracking as the wood dries, the logs were cut on the inside. The notches were made to fit into each other to the exact millimeter in so-called four-point saddle notch joints, so that even in the worst weather conditions the massive Douglas fir logs would stay absolutely tight. The primary ceiling structure was also executed using log construction techniques. The exposed logs were notched and joined with the log walls, thereby strengthening the building structurally. Wood fiber insulation was installed over the rafters of the round log roof. The ceiling beams, also of solid wood, were flattened, leveled off, and joined to the supporting walls as well.

Douglas Fir

The wood of the Douglas fir, a conifer from the pine family, has a high degree of dimensional stability and is very well-suited as a building material. Because of the low moisture content in its heartwood after felling, a maximum of forty percent, there is little shrinkage during the drying process. This in turn results in less cracking and warping. Douglas fir wood is naturally very durable and eminently suited to use in construction. Its heartwood is highly resistant to fungal growth and insect infestation and its glowing reddish color is very attractive. The home's L-shaped stairs with their heartwood-free treads and stair cheeks in the living area, as well as the stair railings, were also all constructed with Douglas fir by the log house builder. Earth-colored porcelain tiles were installed on the lower level floors, while country pine wood plank flooring was selected for the upper level. Large pointed dormers break up the long line of the tiled pitched roof and let light into the upper level.

↖ The two pointed dormers give the home's façade contour and go well with the carefully planned landscaping including its lovely wooden bridge.

← The wide gable of giant logs is balanced and set in context by the flowing stream, the garden landscaping, and the home's stony foundation.

↑ The massiveness of the solid construction is softened by the large windows and the design with exposed beams open to the roof ridge.

↑ Durable and beautiful, the attached kitchen island of natural stone.

Wood Gasification and Solar Thermal Heating

The energy-smart wood gasification heating system with a nominal capacity of 35 kilowatts was placed in the center of the house. In a wood gasification boiler, unlike in a traditional wood stove, the processes of wood gasification and wood combustion take place in two different combustion chambers at different times, that is, separate from each other in time and place. This type of system is very advantageous because it can reach a higher level of efficiency—about ninety percent, while producing very low emissions. A 528 gallon [2,000 liter] combi-buffer storage tank connected to the heating circuit is also fed by a 161-square-foot [15-square-meter] solar array to provide hot water and support the main heating system. Because of this, there is no need to heat the wood gasification unit in the summer to water: the collector heat pipes take care of that. Heat is circulated through the low-energy radiant floor heating system on both floors. The impressive size of the combustion chamber that can accommodate logs of up to 19.7" [50 cm] in length, also provides a great deal of convenience. Even on the coldest winter days, the system only has to be loaded once a day. Furthermore, it can burn cheaper softwoods and scrap wood, which keeps the average annual heating costs down to a manageable $630 [450 EUROS based on 1 EURO = $1.40] per about 494 cubic feet [14 cubic meters]. ●

← Cozy and warm on all sides, the open living area with its heated tile flooring, fireplace, and heat-retaining log walls form the heart of the house.

ℹ A total of approximately **7,063 ft³ [200 m³]** of wood volume was used in construction. This is equivalent to a carbon component in wood of **55 tons [50 metric tons]**, which is equivalent, in turn, to the storage of **201.7 tons [183 metric tons]** of carbon dioxide for 100 years.

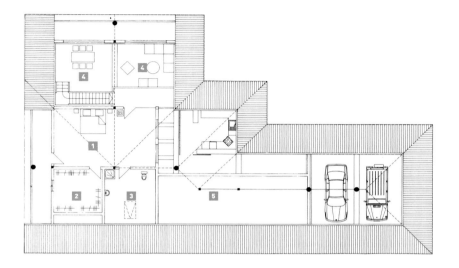

M 1:300

UPPER/LOFT LEVEL

1 MASTER BEDROOM
2 WALK-IN CLOSET
3 BATH
4 GALLERY
5 STORAGE (ACCESS TO GARAGE)

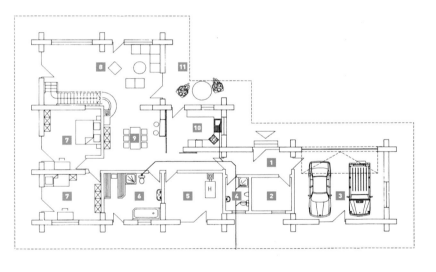

M 1:300

LOWER LEVEL

1 ENTRY
2 STORAGE
3 GARAGE
4 BATH, 3/4
5 UTILITY/MECHANICAL
6 BATH
7 BEDROOM / CHILD
8 LIVING
9 DINING
10 KITCHEN
11 TERRACE

M 1:300 **ELEVATIONS**

MANUFACTURER	CHARLIE MANZ BLOCKHAUSBAU GMBH
ARCHITECT	TIMO MANZ
LOCATION	GERMANY, LOWER SAXONY
LOT SIZE	+/- 52 ACRES [21 HECTARES]
LIVING AREA	4,306 FT² [400 M²]
CONSTRUCTION COSTS	NOT SPECIFIED
COMPLETION	2004

THREE LOG HOME BROTHERS IN THE ALPS

In a small rural community in southern Upper Bavaria, three carpenters follow the log construction path of their forefathers while forging ahead with their own ideas.

This log house, made of locally grown mountain spruce, stands in a wide valley floor with an unobstructed view of the Bavarian alpine landscape. The mountain wood, with its compact growth rings, was felled in the winter and stored for six months before beginning construction. After this resting period of half a year, the wood was dried in a kiln to a residual moisture content of fifteen percent. The handcrafted house is a structure of mixed styles, typical of the region. On top of a concrete basement foundation, a 19.3" [49-cm] thick brick wall was constructed and then covered with lime plaster. Then a second level of solid log construction with a multi-shelled permeable wall structure was set on top of this base. The outer spruce log wall shell is 5.5" [14-cm] thick and is followed by a 3.9" [10-cm] thick wood fiber insulation layer, which is finished off on the interior walls by 1.18" [30-mm] thick spruce cladding.

Refined Surfaces

The log house's exterior walls were upgraded by receiving a special carpentry finish. The north, east, and south sides have completely hewn surfaces. The work was done manually with a cutting device that the craftsmen developed themselves. This gave the walls a fine structure of smooth surfaces that makes them appear both rugged and refined. As a finishing touch, the wood surfaces were also brushed, which separated the early wood from the rest and made the wall even more weather resistant. The western wall, which bears the brunt of the weather's abuse, was clad in split larch shingles, whose long life of up to 100 years is due to their high resin content and the natural durability of coniferous wood. Split larch shingles have been used to clad roofs and façades in Europe for hundreds of years and have stood the test of time very well. The notches were executed precisely and made airtight in the chal-

lenging "Klingschrot" style of the master craftsman, a type of extended full dovetail joint in which distinct patterns are formed by the interlocking log notches.

Wooden Gutters

The round roof gutters were milled and also made of untreated larch wood. Smoothly planed on the outer and inner sides, the gutters are extremely durable and resistant to rot, ice, hail, and snowfall, in addition to being a fine adornment to any log house. Their conically tapering form follows the growth pattern of the larch trunk, producing a natural slope. The roof was constructed as a craftsman-built purlin roof with horizontal rafters. Wood fiber insulation boards with a thickness of 9.4" [24 cm] were installed on the roof. A structural component for the protection of the house's wood exteriors is provided by the wide roof overhang of 7.2' [2.20 m] on the gabled east side, which shelters the wrap-around balcony year-round, and another overhang of 5.9' [1.8 m] on the eaves. Natural clay tiles cover the roof. Wide fir plank flooring was installed throughout the house, except for in the entry area where reclaimed tile was used. The stairway, including its lathed railing, was also made of solid fir wood while the grid windows, which give the alpine log house a friendly look, were crafted of larch wood.

↗ The alpine log house in the mixed style of Upper Bavaria shows traditional carpentry in its purest form.

→ A European tradition for centuries: The side with the greatest exposure to the elements is clad with weatherproof larch wood shingles.

Manufacturing Techniques, Old and New

The interior log walls are 4.7" [12 cm] thick and are joined to the home's exterior walls using the Malschrot method, a traditional regional technique, which like the Klingschrot technique lets the end grain of the interlocking log ends show through the connecting wall to form a flat and flush, decorative pattern where the logs join. These patterns can be quite elaborate. The center of life in this home revolves around the kitchen and living/dining room areas on the first floor. An office and a half-bath are also located on the lower level. On the upper level, there are four bedrooms and a spacious family bath. The home's heating needs are met with a wood chip heating system with a rated capacity of 15 kilowatts that feeds the low-energy radiant floor heating system and provides hot water as well by means of a 211.34 gallon [800 liter] buffer storage tank. The 883 ft3 [25 m3] large storage room for the fully automatically loaded wood chip system is located in the basement. In addition to this, a basic masonry heater in the living area on the first floor with a stated capacity of 5 kilowatts provides comfortable radiant heat. The innumerable details in craftsmanship, which grew out of centuries of carpentry and wood construction tradition, combined with the use of manufacturing devices newly developed by the builders themselves, prove that the three carpenter brothers have brought the traditional art of wood construction into a new age. •

↑ All completely handcrafted from local wood: the staircase, wood plank flooring, walls, and ceilings are of fir wood, while the windows are larch wood.

ℹ A total of approximately **2,825 ft³ [80 m³]** of wood volume was used in construction. This is equivalent to a carbon component in wood of **22 tons [20 metric tons]**, which is equivalent, in turn, to the storage of **80.46 tons [73 metric tons]** of carbon dioxide for 100 years.

MANUFACTURER	GEBRÜDER DUFTER (DUFTER BROTHERS) GMBH
ARCHITECT	SYLVESTER DUFTER
LOCATION	GERMANY, BAVARIA
LOT SIZE	10,764 FT² OR .25 ACRE [1,000 M²]
LIVING AREA	2,153 FT² [200 M²]
CONSTRUCTION COSTS	$392,000 [280,000 EURO]
	BASE OF CALCULATION: 1 EURO = $1.40 USD
COMPLETION	2005

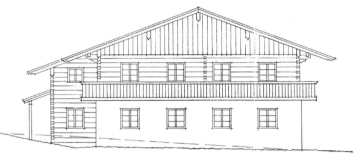

M 1:200 / **ELEVATION**

M 1:200 / **ELEVATION**

M 1:200
LOWER LEVEL
1 ENTRY
2 HALF-BATH
3 OFFICE
4 STORGE
5 GARAGE
6 LIVING/DINING
7 KITCHEN

M 1:200
UPPER LEVEL
1 HALLWAY
2 ROOM
3 BEDROOM / CHILD
4 MASTER BEDROOM
5 WALK-IN CLOSET
6 BATH
7 STORAGE

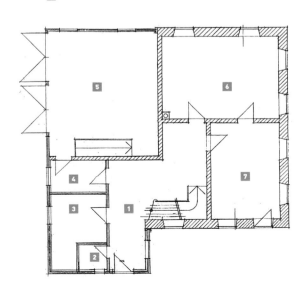

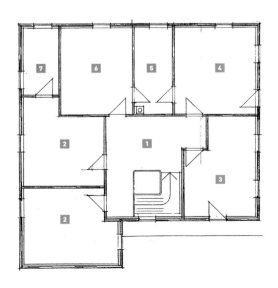

A SYSTEM WITH CONVICTION

In the northwestern part of Lower Saxony in Germany, a Finnish log house unites wood construction traditions with profound manufacturing technology.

This squared-off two-story log house built with Finnish polar pine has a rectangular floor plan and is positioned with its longer side toward the street. Its multi-shelled wall construction is patented and based on the findings of Finnish wood construction research. An additional 5.5" [140-mm] thick layer of cellulose insulation was placed between the inner supporting log wall measuring 3.6" [9.2 cm] and the outer wall cladding of profiled, 1.1" [28 mm] thick pine panels. This cellulose insulation is made from recycled newspaper and blown through a high pressure process into the hollow space between the walls. It not only gives added insulation, it also provides soundproofing. Nevertheless, excess moisture in the indoor air can pass through the inner log wall through the cellulose insulation and on through the outer cladding to the outside without a problem.

Unifying Principle

The wall was constructed deliberately without any type of artificial foils, vapor, or air barriers. Because of this, the wall structure remains open to diffusion like the natural building material wood and the indoor climate of the log house remains healthy. Moreover, the temperature of the surfaces of the solid wood walls matches the air temperature. Since there is no difference between the air and the wall surface temperatures, there are no drafts that could stir up house dust and germs or that could cause respiratory problems. The combined weight of the roof and the upper floor ceiling rests on the supporting log wall and presses its wedge-shaped tongue-and-groove notches together so that no drafts get through. A layer of cellulose insulation, 7.5" [190 mm] thick was also installed on the roof, following the principle of treating the outer wall and

the roof as one unit, so that no thermal bridges are created where the two structural elements meet.

Rational Pre-Fabrication

With computer-aided design (CAD) and computer numerical control (CNC) of milling and manufacturing machines, over ninety percent of the structure can be pre-fabricated. Because of this, the log house could be erected in only 25 days, and completed in only 18 weeks, including the interior work and all installations and connections. The home's center is the living room with its impressive 19' [5.8 m] high ceilings that give the room a feeling of spacious openness reaching all the way up to the gallery on the upper level. The kitchen space flows into the dining area, and a room with a large bay window provides the perfect work space and office in the house's northeastern corner. A custom-built solid wood stairway leads to the upper level that underscores the natural character of the log house with the exposed beams and rafters. The upstairs bathroom with its integrated sauna suits the Finnish way of life. This generously proportioned log home, which has no basement level, is completed by its bedrooms, as well as a second office, kitchen, and living room.

↗ Typically Finnish—compact, friendly, and modest: This log home feels cozy, despite its spacious 2,691 square feet [250 square meters] of living space.

→ Sustainable and healthy: Geothermal heat, natural stone, and polar pine wood.

↑ Extending the upstairs gallery to overlook the living room creates a spacious atmosphere.

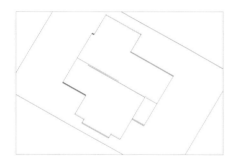

M 1:300 / **CROSS SECTION**

MANUFACTURER	NORDIC HAUS BLOCKHÄUSER
ARCHITECT	FRANZ-JOSEF ROLFSEN
LOCATION	GERMANY, LOWER SAXONY
LOT SIZE	8,170 FT² OR .187 ACRES [759 M²]
LIVING AREA	2,766 FT² [257 M²]
CONSTRUCTION COST	$532,000 [380,000 EURO]
	BASE OF CALCULATION: 1 EURO = $1.40 USD
COMPLETION	2000

M 1:300
UPPER LEVEL
1. GALLERY
2. BATH/SAUNA
3. BEDROOM
4. LIVING
5. WORK/OFFICE
6. BALCONY
7. KITCHEN
8. OPEN TO BELOW

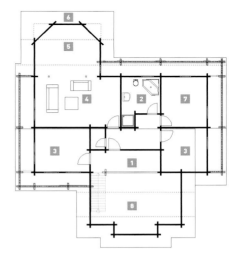

Geothermal Heat and a Masonry Heater

A geothermal heat pump that is connected to ground collector coils, installed horizontally under the ground frost line at a depth of 3.93' [1.20 m], provides the house with heat and hot water. The heat, which produces no emissions, is circulated through the two stories of the home via the low-energy radiant floor heating system. In addition, a powerful masonry heater, with a rated output of 8 kilowatts, installed in the living room, provides toasty heat and a cozy atmosphere. Wide roof overhangs protect the entire structure from driving rain and shelter the balcony that wraps around both floors of the house on its southwestern side from wind and weather. The large thermal windows installed on all sides give the wood construction contour and a welcoming look. The roof, with its 25 degree pitch, gives the Finnish log home continuity in color with its gleaming reddish-brown natural clay tiles. ●

M 1:300
LOWER LEVEL
1. ENTRY
2. DINING
3. KITCHEN
4. WORK/OFFICE
5. LIVING
6. HALF-BATH
7. CLOSET
8. STORAGE

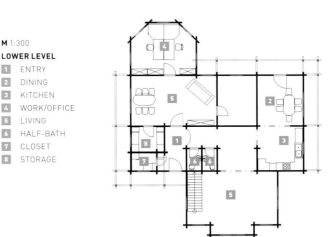

ℹ️ A total of approximately **7,063 ft³ [200 m³]** of wood volume was used in construction. This is equivalent to a carbon component in wood of **55.1 tons [50 metric tons]**, which is equivalent, in turn, to the storage of **201.7 tons [183 metric tons]** of carbon dioxide for 100 years.

A CANADIAN-FRISIAN COMPOSITION

In Tecklenburger Land in Germany, three log-house generations live and work under one very special roof.

On the northern edge of the German federal state of North Rhine-Westphalia right on the border to Lower Saxony, a picturesque bungalow unites Canadian log house craftsmanship with traditional Frisian architecture. The German region of Tecklenburger Land consists largely of the village-like communities of the administrative district of Steinfurt, where the foothills of Teutoburg Forest highlands meet the flat park landscape of the Münsterland region.

Exact Symmetry

This log house, built without a basement level, stands out because of its distinct and unique appearance. Its exact symmetry calls up visions of grand country estates. The residence consists of a rectangular main building of one-and-a-half stories, flanked on either side by one-story wings, one facing north and the other south, with the same plan but different sizes. The pine wood used for construction came from high forest areas and was harvested in the winter in the phase of the new moon and then peeled, or debarked by hand. Wool was inserted as insulation between the logs measuring 13.8" [35 cm] in diameter on average. The stairway and railing in the center section of the house was hand-crafted out of Douglas fir by the log house builder.

Reminiscent of Frisian Architecture

The longer sides of the main house feature three peaked gables that run the entire width of the house from front to back, straight through the pitched roof. The larger, central gable, which forms a sort of peaked cross-tract bisecting the length of the house, creates more space on the upper level and lets in lots of light. The Canadian log house designer elevated the central peaked dormer to create a full-blown peaked gabled roof as a type of reinterpretation of a typical Frisian architectural element. It is located directly over the home's grand entrance door whose wide sheltering canopy roof is supported by two capital columns of wood.

Roman Clay Tiles Fired with Engobe Recipes

The home's tasteful country estate or villa character is underscored by the roofing of Roman clay tiles, whose form is similar to that of a Roman clay half-pipe or canal, hence the name Roman barrel or canal tiles. The tiles were made of all-natural, high-quality clay sintered at 2,012 degrees Fahrenheit [1,100 degrees Celsius]. Through this process of very hot firing, the tiles become frost resistant, color-fast, and very durable. In addition, their finish has a bisque or glazed appearance that gives even newly produced tiles the desirable look of already aged and weathered "old estate" tiles. Since the roof's surface is divided up into separate, defined gutter sections, rain water can run off quickly even on low-pitched roofs. The rich color variations in the clay roofing are due to the fact that the tiles are made with natural, colored liquid clay slips or muds. These so-called engobes are applied to the originally reddish-brown roof tiles shortly before they are fired. During the firing process, they bond inseparably with the tile to produce a permanent, wear-resistant earth or ocher-colored coating.

← Like a fairy-tale, yet so real: The splendor of natural logs builds a home of lasting architectural value.

↑ The ceiling construction, with the exposed round log beams of the flat hip roof, adds a multifaceted accent to the living room.

↑ The circular staircase winding around a natural trunk was hand-crafted from the hard and durable wood of the Douglas fir, also know as the Oregon Pine.

Geothermal Heat Close to the Surface

In the main part of the house, there is a spacious combined living, dining, and kitchen area, all open to the gallery above. The guest half-bath, a home office or work room, and the mechanical/utility room are also located on the first floor of the central section of the house. The upper level provides room for the master bedroom for the parents, two bedrooms for the children, and a large family bathroom. In the somewhat larger southern wing of the home, the family's grandmother has her own ground-level apartment, while an office, an archive room, and another bathroom are located in the northern wing. Flat collectors were laid close to the surface, just 4.9' [1.5 m] underground over an area of 16,146 ft2 or .37 acre [1,500 m2]. The heat pump connected to the collectors draws the geothermal heat from the liquid in the collector system and compresses it. The flow temperature produced in this manner serves the low-energy radiant floor heating on the first floor, which is circulated through an oak plank floor. The heat pump also provides hot water for the home's needs. ●

MANUFACTURER + ARCHITECT	GRAHAM BRUCE OFIELD
LOCATION	GERMANY, TECKLENBURG
PLOT SIZE	27,628 FT2 [8421 M2]
LIVING AREA	1379 FT2 [420 M2]
CONSTRUCTION COSTS	ON REQUEST
COMPLETION	2007

← Previous pages: The log house country estate, with its colorful roofing, is surrounded by a park-like garden, whose natural pond biotope is fed by a rain-water cistern.

↓ The uncluttered and unfussy kitchen creates a comfortable atmosphere with its clear lines.

N ◑ **SITE PLAN**

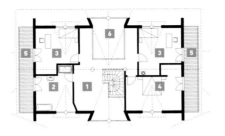

M 1:400 / **UPPER LEVEL**

1 GALLERY	**4** BEDROOM/CHILD
2 BATH	**5** BALCONY
3 BEDROOM/CHILD	**6** OPEN TO BELOW

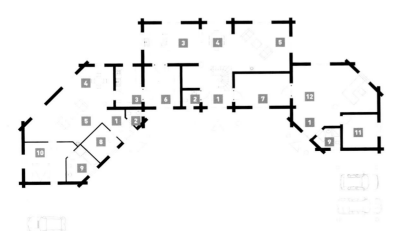

M 1:400 / **LOWER LEVEL**

1 ENTRY	**7** WALK-THROUGH
2 HALF-BATH	**8** CLOSET
3 KITCHEN	**9** BATH
4 DINING	**10** BEDROOM
5 LIVING	**11** STORAGE/ARCHIVE
6 STORAGE	**12** OFFICE

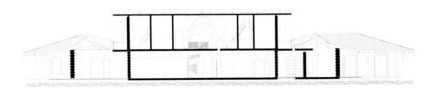

M 1:400 / **ELEVATION**

LOG HOUSE IN AN ENERGY-INDEPENDENT ALPINE COMMUNITY

The combination of the renewable raw material wood with the renewable energy of the sun defines the guiding principles of sustainable tourism in the twenty-first century.

The Tennengebirge mountain range is a rugged, heavily karstified plateau in the Northern Limestone Alps, whose highest peak (Raucheck) rises to 7,972 foot [2,430 meters] over mean sea level. At the feet of this peak, surrounded by imposing steep faces, a small mountain resort town has not forgotten its ancient roots in the region's settlement history. The rural community, about 28 miles [45 kilometers] south of Salzburg, Austria, in the administrative district of Pongau, was the site of early log houses already in the Neolithic Period.

Solar-powered Electricity and Solid Wood Construction

For many years already, the Climate Alliance community located 2,953 feet [900 meters] above sea level has advanced its total concept for sustainability with an intense focus on tourism. The aim of this concept is to achieve a self-sufficient, climate-neutral energy supply. At present, two large solar electric power plants have been installed by private investors with municipal support; this facility represents one of the largest photovoltaic installations in Austria and supplies more than two-thirds of the municipality's households—approximately 700 residents—with decentralized electricity. In addition, the vacation community has an impressive local transportation concept that produces no emissions and very little noise pollution: "electromobiles," or electric cars, along with their charging stations, and biogas driven smart cars are provided free of cost to allow visitors to move around the area without having to have their own private cars. In the winter, horse-drawn sleds are the preferred mode of transporta-

tion because ice-melting salt is not used on the streets for it is harmful to the ground water. One further piece in the greater mosaic-like concept for sustainability is the natural log resort with six houses built in Canadian log house style with the renewable natural resource of wood.

Moose, Black Bear, and Beaver

On the map of the alpine resort's log houses, there are three black bears, one elk, and one beaver, because these native Canadian animals lend their names to the resort's five guest chalets, which differ in size but are similar in style, level of comfort, and furnishings. The one-story "Little Beaver" is an ideal honeymoon lodge, while the "Black Bear," with its two stories, is perfect for families of up to six. The largest lodge, the "Wild Moose," offers five bedrooms and can sleep up to ten. In each log house there is a fully equipped kitchen with a striking natural log bar that also functions as a beautiful room divider. Off the kitchen is the living and dining area with its homey central wood stove and genuine leather sofa for true comfort. Each house also has its own sauna and a wonderful outdoor hot tub with fantastic views of the Tennengebirge mountains to add the finishing touch to this perfect oasis of relaxation. In addition, the separate, sheltered larchwood terraces of each lodge allow guests to enjoy the great outdoors with direct access to all the resort has to offer—hiking trails, climbing paths, and ski trails.

The New Definition of Luxury

In the reception building constructed with the wood of local silver fir, along with the reception desk, guests will find a large, sheltered grill area, a panorama terrace, and a rustic pub that offers all-natural, organic products from the region. Nature and quality of life have found each other in this spot. The term "luxury" gets a whole new meaning here: undisturbed peace and tranquility, a breathtaking mountain world that has been left intact, the ambiance of primitive beauty in the solid wood log houses, clean air,

← A Canadian log house at 3,281 feet [1,000 meters] in the Alps..

120

← As in the home, so in the bedroom: harmony, peace, and warmth in a log bed for two.

↑ The vacation village consists of five chalets, or log lodges, with different layouts and features..

→ Spectacular views of the Alps from the stunning gable windows of the loft level and the larch wood terrace, sheltered from the wind.

N **SITE PLAN**

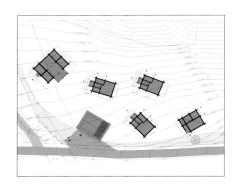

M 1:200
LOWER LEVEL
1 ENTRY
2 LIVING
3 DINING
4 KITCHEN
5 BEDROOM
6 BATH
7 SAUNA

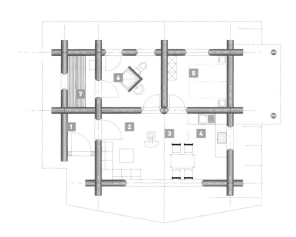

122

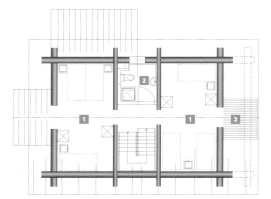

M 1:200
UPPER LEVEL
1 BEDROOM
2 3/4 BATH
3 BALCONY

M 1:200 / **CROSS SECTION**

M 1:200
LOWER LEVEL

1	ENTRY	6	STORAGE
2	CLOSET	7	BEDROOM
3	BATH	8	DINING
4	HALF-BATH	9	LIVING
5	SAUNA	10	KITCHEN

M 1:200
LOWER LEVEL
1 ENTRY
2 CLOSET
3 SAUNA
4 3/4 BATH
5 HALF-BATH
6 KITCHEN
7 DINING
8 LIVING
9 TERRACE

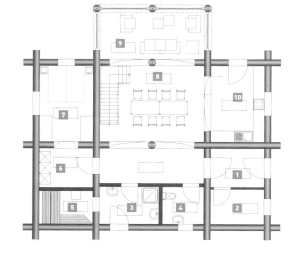

M 1:200 / **ELEVATION**

MANUFACTURER + ARCHITECT	TEAM KANADABLOCKHAUS GMBH
LOCATION	AUSTRIA, SALZBURG
LOT SIZE	64,583 FT² OR 1.48 ACRES [6,000 M²]
LIVING AREA	6,307.6 FT² [586 M²]
CONSTRUCTION COST	NOT SPECIFIED
COMPLETION	2009

↑ The definition of cozy comfort: the fire glowing in the solidly sturdy log house living room.

↑ Particularly delightful: enjoying the breathtakingly beautiful, panoramic views under the open skies.

and clear water. While the moose and the beaver lodges were built with spruce from Karelia, Finland, the black bear lodges were built of northern pine.

Pellets and Masonry Heaters

The walls on the ground levels of the chalet houses were constructed with massive natural logs measuring on average 15″ [38 cm] across. On top of this log construction base, either another full log story was placed as in the bear lodge or a timber frame construction was built, as in the moose lodge, whose exterior walls were constructed with a floor-to-ceiling cladding of regional pine. The soaring ceilings of the ground levels of all the lodges, and the 38-degree slope of the moose lodge's steeply pitched roof with its cross ridge, as well as the gallery area with its full walls of windows create a feeling of openness in the interiors. A fully automatically controlled pellet heating system with a rated output of 58 kilowatts provides the log house vacation village with heat and hot water. The pellet storage unit is located on the basement level of the main building and measures 989 ft3 [28 m3]. Two buffer storage tanks, each with a capacity of 528.3 gallons [2,000 liters] are connected to the low-energy radiant floor heating systems. The masonry heaters in the chalets serve two purposes: they heat the solid wood buildings in the seasons when the main heating system is not in operation and they provide guests with unforgettable log-house ambiance. ●

ℹ️ A total of approximately **17,481 ft³ [495m³]** of wood volume was used in construction. This is equivalent to a carbon component in wood of **135.6 tons [123 metric tons]**, which is equivalent, in turn, to the storage of **499.3 tons [453 metric tons]** of carbon dioxide for 100 years.

MARITIME PERSPECTIVES

In Mecklenburg-Vorpommern, or Mecklenburg-Western Pomerania, the federal state in the north of Germany on the Baltic coast, a log house inn charms visitors between the old seaside resorts of Warnemünde and Heiligendamm.

Surrounded by endless meadows, shady tree-lined boulevards, and secluded beaches, the inn located directly by the sea awaits its guests in need of rest and relaxation. Built to last, this natural log house fits in well with the style of the local manor houses and country estates with their historically landmarked barns and thatched roofs. Indeed, the solid wood log house style truly complements the original charm of the old fishing and farming village.

Thuringian High Forest Spruce

The inn's 130-year-old spruce logs all come from the same tree crop harvested from the high forest areas of Germany's ancient Thuringian Forest, which lies at 1,969 feet [600 meters] above sea level. Each tree was inspected for problematic spiral growth and felled in winter in the phase before new moon. Then, the logs were peeled, or debarked, using high pressure water. The hand-scraped logs, 70 in number, have an average diameter of 15.75" [40 cm]. In total, the log house consists of eight log courses with an exterior inferior purlin as the ninth course. While saddle notches were used for the log walls, dovetail notches without projecting edges were used for the ceiling beams.

← The log house inn shows its close connection to its natural surroundings in all its loving details.

One-of-a-Kind Log House

The gable front, which is exposed to the elements, is perfectly protected by dark black slate. In addition, wide roof overhangs of 5.91' [1.8 m] on all sides protect the entire construction from the weather. A discreet green was chosen for the roofing on the compact structure. Key features of the building are the natural log columns placed for support both on the outside and inside. The addition of these strikingly rugged elements makes for a log house experience that is not only a pleasure to look at but a pleasure to touch. A side addition, with a slightly pitched flat roof and two bays in post and beam construction, opens up the building's sturdy appearance. The interior walls on the lower level were constructed using the natural log method as well, while on the upper level, dry construction techniques with qualified soundproofing and insulation were employed to provide some design variation.

Well-planned Energy Concept

The natural stone fireplace centrally located in the large breakfast and common gathering room weighs over 2.2 tons [2 metric tons] and has a rated output of 4 kilowatts. Because of the enormous storage capacity of the stones, the large fireplace structure heats up very slowly. The heat stored up inside the fireplace is released gradually and can heat the surrounding rooms for up to two days without having to fire the combustion chamber again. Because of the open construction concept between the lower and upper levels, the large fireplace keeps the log house warm throughout the heating season. The solid wood walls also absorb, store, and release heat again slowly into the space as the room temperature sinks. In addition, an economical condensing gas boiler, connected to the low-energy radiant floor heating system on the first story, ensures the inn's heating supply. In total, the log house inn has six double rooms, each of which features its own bath and kitchenette and individually adjustable heat and hot water.

← Natural stone and rugged log columns underscore the originality of the Baltic Sea inn..

126

← The side addition with its gently sloping flat roof and its bays loosens up the overall architectural composition.

→ The restful inn rooms with their simple but tasteful décor.

→ Cozy and warm: the crackling fire in the natural stone fireplace and the natural spruce trunks of the spacious common room.

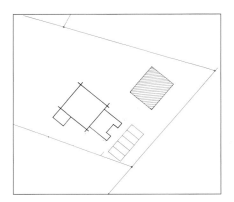

MANUFACTURER	LÖFFLER NATURSTAMMHAUS GMBH & CO. KG
ARCHITECT	UTE BALDAUF
LOCATION	GERMANY, MECKLENBURG-VORPOMMERN
LOT SIZE	10,764 FT², OR .25 ACRE [1,000 M²]
LIVING AREA	2,260 FT² [210 M²]
CONSTRUCTION COST	$280,000 [200,000 EURO]
	BASE OF CALCULATION: 1 EURO = $1.40 USD
COMPLETION	2009

Nature, Culture, and Organic Cooking

Following their own personal principles, the nature-loving owners and innkeepers place their focus on an overall ecological concept in the great outdoors. For this reason, the inn features its own Finnish sauna with a relaxation area and an invitingly restful and spacious 431 square feet [40 sqaure meters] terrace of Douglas fir. Rainwater is collected in a cistern and is used to water the flowers and vegetable beds in the garden. Visitors sleep in hand-crafted natural log beds in the individually designed guest rooms. The four units on the upper level are designed with families in mind and have extra space on the finished gabled attic level that can be reached via a pull-down ladder. In the inn's own kitchen, all-natural meals are prepared using only organic products from the region. ●

ℹ A total of approximately **6,357 ft³ [180m³]** of wood volume was used in construction. This is equivalent to a carbon component in wood of **49.6 tons [45 metric tons]**, which is equivalent, in turn, to the storage of 181.9 tons [**165 metric tons**] of carbon dioxide for 100 years.

M 1:200 / **ELEVATION**

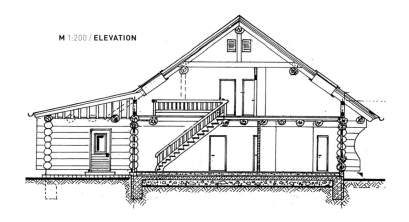

↗ Solid wood log walls alternate with smooth surfaces on the upper level.

→ Two things guarantee a good night's rest: the fresh Baltic Sea air and the hand-crafted natural log bed.

JEWEL ON THE PALATINATE WINE ROUTE

Among the vineyards and the orchards, a log house on the edge of Germany's Palatinate Forest testifies to the union of man and nature.

This spruce log house of one and a half stories has an L-shaped floor plan. The wood, dense because of its slow growth, came from mountainous Alpine regions over 2,625 feet [800 meters] above sea level. The core-separated logs, felled in winter, were stored for six months in order to dry them in a drying chamber, or kiln, to a residual moisture content of fifteen percent before using them for construction. The ground level, including the knee wall, was constructed from a fourfold, tongue-and-groove, solid spruce log wall system with a thickness of 7.9" [20 cm]. The squared-off log beams consist of three laminated layers, whereby the resistant heartwood forms the outer layer. Problems with warping and settling are avoided by using laminated log wood. The upper level was built using timber-frame construction methods. The hollow space within the wood frame was insulated with a breathable and permeable wood fiber layer of 7.9" [20 cm] in thickness. Outside and inside, the framework was covered with 1.06" [27 mm] spruce planks to maintain the home's log house character.

Dovetail Notch

The joints were executed as dovetail notches. With these tight, high-quality joints, the slanted tongues of the individual log courses produce very clean edges. The interior layout of the log house—whose interior walls are also constructed of 3.9" [10 cm] thick solid wood walls—is defined by two larger main living spaces on both the lower and the upper level. Next to the foyer on the first floor, the kitchen and dining room are connected and simultaneously divided by a beautiful and practical counter bar unit. From the kitchen area, a stairway leads to the basement level. The stairway is housed in an eye-catching and space-saving bay set into the inner corner of the floor plan. The bright and spacious sunken living room with 10.5' [3.2 m] high ceilings is located on a slightly lower level. A small guest bedroom and a three-quarter bath complete the first floor.

Exposed Construction

An L-shaped solid beech wood stairway leads from the living room to the open gallery area above. A generously proportioned bedroom and spacious office/studio are located on the upper level under the gables. Both rooms have their own balconies, which are sheltered by the wide overhang of the roof gable in the bedroom and by a dormer construction in the office. The comfortable family bathroom is located in the northern corner of the log house. Both the ceiling structure and the studio roof truss, insulated by a wood fiber panel, were constructed with exposed, core-separated spruce beams. Reddish-brown clay tiles were installed on the saddle roof with its cross gable and 35 degree pitch.

Pellet Stove and Solar-powered Heating

One-hundred-year-old reclaimed terra cotta tiles that once adorned an old palace were installed in the living room. In the rest of the log house, wide spruce and larch plank flooring was installed. The sun-drenched terrace is located outside in the southwestern corner formed by two sides of the log house and sheltered from the wind. Accessible from either the living room or the dining room, the terrace, with its invitingly comfortable atmosphere, calls to mind the inner courtyard of the old, dilapidated farm house that once stood on that spot. The stones gathered

↗ The L-shaped, solid wood log house construction is rich in variation with its two balconies, bay window, and landscape design.

→ Completely sheltered and nestled against the house, the stone-flagged terrace is in a sunny corner.

← Flowing room transitions with sophisticated interior design. The masonry heater located in the center of the terra cotta tiled living room frames the L-shaped stairway to the open gallery area above.

↓ The combined kitchen and dining area, with its colorful countertop bar, makes an impression with its well-balanced concept and friendly design..

from the ruins of the old farmhouse were used to build a wall to enclose the herb and vegetable garden. The heating needs of the log house are met through a modular concept: a fully automatic pellet stove with a rated output of 14 kilowatts feeds the low-energy radiant floor heating on both stories and also heats water for use. In addition, a 97-square-foot [9-square-meter] solar thermal heating system and a 181.6 gallon [800 liter] buffer storage tank ensure the hot water supply outside the heating season. The masonry heater, with its output of 10 kilowatts, is centrally located in the living room to supply the log home with basic heat and create an ambiance of natural comfort. •

i A total of approximately **2,472 ft³ [70m³]** of wood volume was used in construction. This is equivalent to a carbon component in wood of **19.3 tons [17.5 metric tons],** which is equivalent, in turn, to the storage of **70.5 tons [64 metric tons]** of carbon dioxide for 100 years.

MANUFACTURER	REMS-MURR-HOLZHAUS GMBH
DESIGN	JÜRGEN RUBASCH
LOCATION	GERMANY, RHINELAND-PALATINATE
LOT SIZE	7,395 FT², OR .17 ACRE [687 M²]
LIVING AREA	1,873 FT² [174 M²]
CONSTRUCTION COST	NOT SPECIFIED
COMPLETION	2007

N ◑ SITE PLAN

M 1:300 **/ CROSS SECTION**

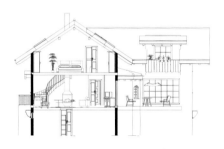

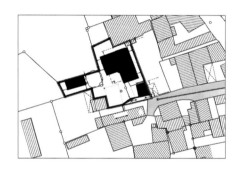

M 1:300
BASEMENT LEVEL
1 FUEL STORAGE
2 HEATING
3 UTILITY/MECHANICAL
4 STORAGE

M 1:300
GROUND LEVEL
1 ENTRY
2 KITCHEN
3 DINING
4 LIVING
5 GUEST BEDROOM
6 3/4 BATH
7 TERRACE

M 1:300
LOFT LEVEL
1 BEDROOM
2 BATH
3 GALLERY
4 OFFICE/STUDIO

THE TRAUNSTEIN LOG HOME TRADITION

The Chiemgau region of Germany in southeastern Bavaria, close to the Austrian border, has a long-standing log house construction tradition with its own unique style.

Both the architectural concept and the construction planning were carried out by this experienced family-run operation. The two-story rectangular log house was built on a gently sloping lot surrounded by the 6,562 foot [2,000 meter] high mountains of the Upper Bavarian Alps. The spruce, fir, and larch wood used for construction comes from selected mountain regions of the Chiemgau at an elevation of about 3,281 feet [1,000 meters] and was felled in winter in the phase before new moon. The beams for the log wall were core-separated, that is, separated in two lengthwise along the wood grain, stored, and air dried for nine months before they were used for construction. The log house builders, carpenters, silviculturists, foresters, and mill workers of this region, rich in wood-working traditions, banded together to form a regional forest and wood management group. Through this initiative, regional wood, grown and harvested following the principles of sustainable forestry, may be verified as having been processed directly by local companies. The focus here is on ensuring short transportation and processing chains, as well as emphasizing ecological and economic aspects.

Traunsteiner Mountain House

Following their own particular passion, the builders constructed the log house as a so-called Traunsteiner mountain house. With its entryways on its longer, or eave, side and its three larger rooms, the log house features a layout that is historically traditional for the farmhouses of this region. In "olden times," a work area with a stall and a barn was located behind the living area. The home has a reinforced concrete foundation with a basement level under two-thirds of its area. On this foundation, a 19.3" [49 cm] thick wall of insulating natural bricks was constructed and then covered with a layer of thermal insulating plas-

ter. A single-shell rectangular spruce wall system with a wall thickness of 6.3" [16 cm] was built on top of this lower level. The roof was constructed as a purlin roof truss with rafters and sheathed with gray engobed, or glazed, interlocking tiles. All of the construction work was planned and executed autonomously, including the stairway with ashwood steps, the spruce stair railing, windows, as well as the interior and exterior doors. The main entrance door was made of solid oak.

Patented "Klingschrot" Joint Milling Machine

Wide roof overhangs of 6.6' [2 meters] protect the three-sided, wrap-around balcony, typical for the region, from the elements all year round. The balcony railing designed specifically to hold plant containers was made of spruce, but the balcony sill, supports, and floor were all constructed of weatherproof larch wood. In the interior, Jura limestone tiles were selected solely for the entry area. In the rest of the house, self-made, fir wood plank flooring of an unusual thickness of 2" [5 cm] was laid—for a floor that will last hundreds of years. The construction of the upper story ceiling consists of ceiling batten, an 8.7" [22 cm] thick layer of wood fiber insulation, a layer of dolomite sand, and the floor planks, which, in this combination, keep leaks and impact noises to a minimum. Another testament to the almost 120 years of professional experience gained by this family company of master craftsmen over five generations is the milling machine for producing precise, decorative notches that join interior walls to exterior walls in the traditional "klingschrot" method of the region. This machine was conceived and built in the company's own metalworking shop and has even been patented. The angled wedges of the

↗ The traditional Traunstein mountain farmhouse has doors along the length of both sides and a wrap-around balcony with flower-pot railings that are sheltered from the elements throughout the year by wide roof overhangs.

notch's connecting pieces create airtight and secure joints in the log walls. In keeping with age-old, woodworking tradition, the klingschrot notches, also known as the Tyrolean leaf, are elegantly curved and precisely flush.

Two Air-Source Heat Pumps

Because of the stony ground on the building lot, the energy concept for this house relies on a dual system with two air heat pumps. The more powerful heat pump provides the house with heat, which is circulated through a low-energy radiant floor heating system on all the floors. The second heat pump provides hot water through a separately piped system throughout the year. This separation is not only very efficient, but it also saves energy in the warm months when no heat is needed. The classic masonry heater in the family room, which provides the space with cozy heat with its rated output of 8 kilowatts, is typical of traditional Traunstein farmhouse décor.●

136

ℹ A total of approximately **5,650 ft³ [160 m³]** of wood volume was used in construction. This is equivalent to a carbon component in wood of **44 tons [40 metric tons]**, which is equivalent, in turn, to the storage of **161 tons [146 metric tons]** of carbon dioxide for 100 years.

MANUFACTURER + ARCHITECT	VINZENZ BACHMANN
LOCATION	GERMANY, BAVARIA
LOT SIZE	13,993 FT², OR .32 ACRE [1,300 M²]
LIVING AREA	2,906 FT² [270 M²]
CONSTRUCTION COST	$560,000 [400,000 EURO]
	BASE OF CALCULATION: 1 EURO = $1.40 USD
COMPLETION	2010

← The hand-crafted stairway connects the brick-walled lower level with the upper level built in log-house construction style.

↑ An example of the highest quality workmanship in carpentry: the flower-pot railing sill sits atop distinctive brackets made of larch wood.

↓ The length of the building faces the sun; inside, three rooms are lined up to catch the rays.

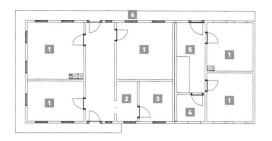

M 1:300
UPPER LEVEL
1 BEDROOM
2 ANTEROOM
3 BATH
4 3/4 BATH
5 HALL
6 BALCONY

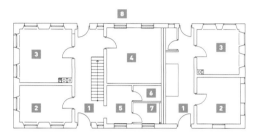

M 1:300   N
LOWER LEVEL
1 ENTRY
2 KITCHEN
3 LIVING
4 ROOM
5 ANTEROOM
6 PANTRY/STORAGE
7 3/4 BATH
8 TERRACE/GARDEN

M 1:300 / **EAST ELEVATION**

M 1:300 / **SOUTH ELEVATION**

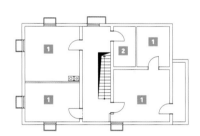

M 1:300
BASEMENT LEVEL
1 BASEMENT
2 HEATING

↓ The traditional center of family life: the cozy living, dining and family room with its wooden, cushioned benches and the masonry heater crafted by a master stove builder.

SELF-SUFFICIENT IN EASTERN WHITE CEDAR

In the wide-open spaces of Germany's northeastern lowlands, a climate-neutral concept log house strives for independence.

The Mecklenburg Switzerland Nature Park [Naturpark Mecklenburgische Schweiz] is located in the heart of the German federal state of Mecklenburg-Vorpommern, or Mecklenburg-Western Pomerania. Up out of the flat landscape of the moraines that lie just a bit above sea level rise gently rolling hills formed in the last ice age. This land of forests and lakes is known for its agricultural and silvicultural importance, its villages untouched by time, its palaces, country manors, and expansive parks.

Residential Home, Model Home, and Company Headquarters

In the midst of the nature park, a log house builder and constructional biologist has created his own special residence and model home, which also functions as his company headquarters. The log house constructed with squared-off log beams of eastern white cedar offers 1,701 square feet [158 square meters] of space on one-and-a-half levels. The interior walls, built using brick and lightweight construction techniques and plastered in cob, a combination of earth and straw, set distinct design counterpoints. The plaster, like the solid log wall, supports a consistently regulated moisture and heat balance within the building. While the residential section with its large windows was systematically planned to face south, the saddle roof lo-

cated over the garage on the street-facing north side of the building was elongated outward. This design element gives greater protection to the side that is more exposed to the elements and improves the effectiveness of the insulation. The logs used for construction come from sustainable forestry sources. The wood was felled in winter in the phase before new moon and is largely free of cracks and warping. Moreover, eastern white cedar wood has a high thermal insulation value, which means that log houses built with it can be constructed with one shell, since they do not require any additional insulation.

Thuja Occidentalis

Eastern white cedar, also known as Arborvitae or American Arborvitae, is not a real cedar but a conifer in the cypress family. It is mainly found in eastern Canada and the northeastern region of the United States around the Great Lakes. The wood of the eastern white cedar is relatively light in weight but very sturdy; its growth is slow and continuous. In addition, it is very weather resistant, undergoes very little shrinkage during the drying process and possesses a natural defense—in its cells there is an essential oil called thujaplicin that prevents pest and insect infestation, as well as fungal growth. For this reason, it is not necessary to apply extra protective wood treatments. In color, the wood is similar to pine and, with its aromatic scent, it creates a warm and comfortable atmosphere.

The End of the Era of Fossil Fuels

The demand for an independent lifestyle has found its logical conclusion in the choice of a modular energy concept. Photovoltaic units with an output of 2.2 kilowatts were installed on the pitched roof and on the south-facing house façade, covering an area of 237 square feet [22 square meters], and produce 2,000 kilowatts per hour on average annually. A solar-powered system with 54 square feet [5 square meters] of flat-plate collectors feeds a 92.5 gallon [350 liter] storage tank to supply hot water. On the home's

↖ A concept for the future of log house design: the self-sufficient home built of arborvitae, or eastern white cedar, with its own supply of electricity from wind and solar energy.

← Following the sun: The terrace, winter garden, and natural herb garden were all precisely designed to face the sun.

↑ The massive masonry heater in the center of the energy-independent log house provides both the lower and upper levels with long-lasting, healthy heat.

← Enter this cozy bedroom and leave stress and noise behind.

rooftop, a wind-power unit produces 330 watts per hour at a wind speed of 19.7 feet [6 meters] per second (or 13.4 miles per hour [21.6 kilometers per hour]). Any surplus energy produced by the solar or wind powered systems is loaded in a battery made of large accumulators located under the roof. Rainwater is collected in a cistern for use in the home's kitchen garden and washing machine. Logical-

ly, two ecological composting toilets complete the total energy concept. The log house, which meets eighty percent of its own energy needs, is very nearly energy independent. The era of fossil fuels such as coal, oil, and gas is already coming to an end in this home.

A brick masonry heater with an output of 7 kilowatts was handcrafted by a stove builder and placed in the center of the log house. Its slow-burning radiant heat warms both the home's lower level and the upper loft level. Because of its enormous storage capacity, the heater provides heat for twenty hours longer after the fire in the combustion chamber has gone out. The floor plan groups the rooms around the masonry heater for maximum energy efficiency. Eleven tons [ten metric tons] of sand were layered in the ceiling construction as insulation. This layer of sand absorbs the heat rising from the central heater and slowly releases it again into the upstairs rooms. All of the exterior walls, the garage, three gables, the terrace, the balcony, and the winter garden were built with the wood of eastern white cedar. This concept log house sets new benchmarks for architectural sustainability.●

N ◓ SITE PLAN

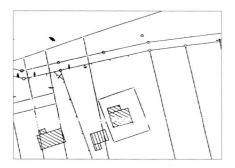

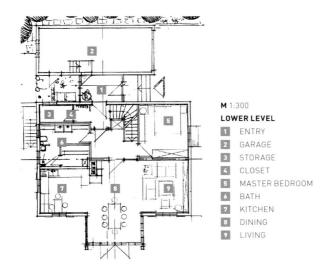

M 1:300
LOWER LEVEL
1 ENTRY
2 GARAGE
3 STORAGE
4 CLOSET
5 MASTER BEDROOM
6 BATH
7 KITCHEN
8 DINING
9 LIVING

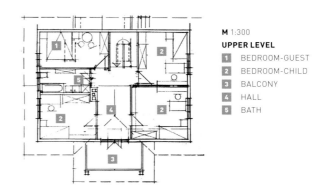

M 1:300
UPPER LEVEL
1 BEDROOM-GUEST
2 BEDROOM-CHILD
3 BALCONY
4 HALL
5 BATH

ℹ A total of approximately **2,472 ft³ [70 m³]** of wood volume was used in construction. This is equivalent to a carbon component in wood of 19.3 tons **[17.5 metric tons]**, which is equivalent, in turn, to the storage of 70.5 tons **[64 metric tons]** of carbon dioxide for 100 years.

MANUFACTURER	FISCHER HOLZBAU GMBH
ARCHITECT	LUTZ KÖHNLEIN
LOCATION	GERMANY, MECKLENBURG-VORPOMMERN
LOT SIZE	13,993 FT², OR .32 ACRE [1,300 M²]
LIVING AREA	1,701 FT² [158 M²]
CONSTRUCTION COST	$386,400 [276,000 EURO]
	BASE OF CALCULATION: 1 EURO = $1.40 USD
COMPLETION	1997

SWISS PRECISION

In central Switzerland, the country's plateau region, a natural log house fulfills its owners' every wish down to the very last detail.

The ancient land of the Celts, the Swiss Jura, which lies to the northwest of the main chain of the Alps, is a range of folded mountains—formed when the earth's crust folded and rose upward because of compressional forces. The Schweizer Mittelland is bordered to the northwest by this ridge, which is known among other things for its towering forests.

Great Prospects

This one-and-a-half story log house was built at an elevation of 2,953 feet [900 meters]. The home's southern side commands expansive views of the region known as the Drei-Seen-Land, or the land of three lakes, all the way to the majestic mountain peaks of the Central Alps. The rectangular base form of its layout is extended to the side by an addition, which is mainly used to house the utility rooms. The walls are constructed with nine courses of silver fir logs, which were felled in winter in the region's forests. After a short drying period for the logs over the summer, construction began in the fall. Each of the logs used for construction, with an average diameter of 15.7" [40 cm], was selected, peeled, and scraped or planed by hand. The house, built without a basement, completely meets the owners' expectations. The clearly defined floor plan and the design concept, which features large spaces open to the gallery, reflect the owners' own free and open lifestyle. The owners' style preferences lean toward architecture closely tied to nature, energy-efficient construction methods without ornate fussiness, and carpentry marked by Swiss precision.

Log House Partner: Wool

The log house builder and master carpenter was personally responsible for the production of the windows, doors, and terrace, as well as several of the one-of-a-kind furniture pieces. For the insulation material on the roof, he chose wool, which has outstanding insulating and sound-proofing properties because of its high gross density. Sheep's wool is a naturally renewable raw material, whose processing requires only a tenth of the energy needed for the production of artificial insulation materials. Moreover, this natural material is easy to process and lasts for an almost indefinite period of time. Like the solid log wall, wool is breathable and hygroscopic. Without any reduction in its effectiveness as an insulation material, wool can absorb up to thirty percent of its own weight in moisture and release it again as needed into the environment. Furthermore, wool can remove a certain amount of contaminants and irritants from the air, which, in turn, contributes to a healthy interior climate. As an insulation material for the space between the roof rafters, wool conforms perfectly to the uneven contours of the wood construction, thereby preventing the formation of heat bridges.

A Soapstone Stove

One solitary, but centrally located, Finnish soapstone stove heats the entire log house. The heat stored by this stove with a total weight of over 1.1 ton [1 metric ton] in one hour of operation amounts to 60 kilowatts per hour. This type of stove burns a large amount of hardwood and excess air at one time at a temperature of over 1,830 degrees Fahrenheit [1,000 degrees Celsius] while producing very few pollutants. The high combustion temperatures speed up the heat storage process, so that the daily period of

↗ Possible in Switzerland: The design, submission plans, and construction were all executed by the master carpenter and home builder

→ The partially sheltered terrace and its furniture, all of heat-treated white fir, were also made by the vendor.

active combustion is only about two hours, which keeps the amount of firewood needed to heat the home low. The stove is made exclusively of dense, heavy soapstone, which can store large amounts of heat. After combustion is complete, it slowly releases heat continuously for a period of up to twenty-four hours. The soapstone stove has found its perfect match in a log home, since wood—used in large volumes in its construction—also has the ability to absorb a great amount of heat and release it again as needed. In this way, the wood used to construct the home also acts as an additional, natural heat reservoir.

Healthy Radiant Heat

The soapstone stove releases heat over a long period of time. This slow release warms the walls, furnishings, ceilings, and floors, which, in turn, release heat again into the room. This creates a healthy and pleasant interior climate, since it is not the air itself that is being heated. When moisture remains in the air, occupants are less likely to get sick and skin and air passages are less likely to get dried out. Moreover, because of the lower relative temperature of the warm surfaces, there is hardly any air movement that can stir up dust, bacteria, and germs like conventional convection heating systems with their hot radiators and heaters can. The already uniquely pleasant interior climate of the log house is perfectly accentuated through the healthy, long-lasting radiant heat. The soapstone stove works at eighty-eight percent efficiency, which means that the combustion chamber only needs to be reloaded once or twice even on a cold winter's day. When wood is burned, less than one percent of its content remains as ash, and even this can be used in the garden as a fertilizer. ●

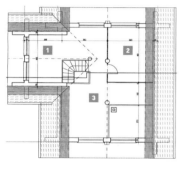

M 1:300
UPPER LEVEL
1 WORK
2 BEDROOM
3 GALLERY

M 1:300
LOWER LEVEL
1 ENTRY
2 BATH
3 KITCHEN
4 UTILITY/MECHANICAL
5 DINING
6 LIVING
7 TERRACE

→ The slowly released radiant heat of the soapstone stove can easily reach the gallery level above through the open-concept design of the log house.

↘ Arches grace the living area and break up the solid architecture with rooms that flow into one another.

M 1:300 / **ELEVATION**

MANUFACTURER	DANYS LOG HOME
ARCHITECT	DANIEL WÜTHRICH
LOCATION	SWITZERLAND, CANTON OF BERN
LOT SIZE	12,917 FT², OR .30 ACRE [1,200 M²]
LIVING AREA	1,937.5 FT² [180 M²]
CONSTRUCTION COST	$378,000 [270,000 EURO]
	BASE OF CALCULATION: 1 EURO = $1.40 USD
COMPLETION	2007

ℹ A total of approximately **4,237.8 ft³ [120 m³]** of wood volume was used in construction. This is equivalent to a carbon component in wood of **33 tons [30 metric tons],** which is equivalent, in turn, to the storage of **121.2 tons [110 metric tons]** of carbon dioxide for 100 years.

HARDWOOD PROTOTYPE ON THE REIAT

Young architects revolutionize solid wood construction in this log house of oak and beech in the Swiss canton of Schaffhausen, near the German border.

The Reiat is a region of gently rolling hills in northern Switzerland perched at an elevation of 1,969 feet [600 meters] above sea level. Among the fields, meadows, extensive mixed woods, and vineyards, a magnificent view expands across the Swiss Plateau, or Swiss Mitteland, all the way to the Alps. In the midst of this rural peacefulness, the renovation of what was once the residence hall of a country school is offering new approaches to building with wood.

Home-grown Hardwood

In solid wood construction, softwood species like fir, spruce, Douglas fir, and pine are commonly used, since costly hardwood is considered to be too expensive and too difficult to work with because of its hardness and weight. However, in this situation things have taken a different turn as a result of a special set of circumstances. When this former school vacation residence was due for an overhaul, the owner weighed the option of using the wood from the property's own forest. With this idea in mind, the owner, a farmer and educator, found innovative architects who could develop a viable overall concept for this particular project. Following the principles of sustainable forestry, he felled some oak and beech trees in November 2007 in the phase before new moon. The hardwood that would normally be used for firewood or timber was instead made into high-quality construction wood. The green trunk wood was cut into beams, planks, and boards with a portable bandsaw directly on the construction site, taking into consideration calculated shrinkage.

← A groundbreaking mix of historical awareness and construction skill: This building may very well shape the style and set the tone for future solid wood construction.

Even tree trunks with smaller diameters could be cut to produce a beam.

The Key: Core Drilling

A crucial pre-condition for the utilization of oak and beech wood for construction purposes was the technique of core drilling. In a process developed exclusively by a local machine building company, the beams were core-drilled right through their length without first having to be sawn. By drilling a beam from both ends with a drill measuring 8.5' [2.6 m] in length, a drilled beam measuring 16' 10" [5.2 m] could be produced. Core drilling significantly shortens the drying phase for dense hardwood, without causing shrinkage cracks. In addition, the process makes the wood stronger, which in turn makes it easier to work with. The degree of residual moisture in the wood needed for construction—namely sixteen percent—was attained in two consecutive phases: first, the wood was air dried for eight months and then it was dried in a vacuum kiln for three weeks. Larger construction areas with longer measurements were handled by means of a tried and true method: the individual, core-drilled beams were lengthened with strong stainless steel connecting rods, so that they could traverse the entire length of the wall of the story under construction, as they do in timber framing.

Pre-Fabrication of System Elements

With computer-aided design (CAD), planners were able to maximize the utilization of pre-fabricated individual system elements. The squared oak beams for the frame construction were sawn to the measurement of 7.9" x 7.9" [20 x 20 cm] and the beech beams for the ceiling construction were cut to a measurement of 10.2" x 10.2" [26 x 26 cm]. For the pine planks of the infill elements, a thickness of 3.9" [10 cm] was sufficient, since they were also insulated with a 6.3" [16 cm] layer of wood wool or excelsior. The manufacturing and the construction were handed over to a wood construction company and a carpenter specialized in log

↑ The term loggia comes from the Italian for loge, compartment, or lodging. In this vacation residence hall, the guests lodge behind lattice-work oak elements, which form the structural and stylistic means of creating an area of shade that playfully combines light and reflection.

→ It is not surprising that people of all tastes, generations, and backgrounds are fans of this solid wood construction..

house construction. The building was erected with exacting precision in just a few days because of the perfectly prefabricated individual modules. Timber construction, though closely related to traditional log construction, nevertheless does not share log construction's problems with structural settling. In timber frame construction, building loads are completely absorbed by the outer load-bearing structure.

Unity of Life and Value Benefit

The timber frame structure with its modular concept faces southwest and stands on a concrete basement foundation, on which three full stories were built using timber construction techniques. On the basement level, there are toilets, a natural cellar with round gravel flooring used as a storeroom, two storage rooms, and a technical room. The first floor is a multifunctional space with the rooms functioning as dining rooms, conference or breakout rooms, a restaurant on the weekends, as well as a seminar room with a professional kitchen including a buffet. On the two floors above, there are six living room/bedroom units for the young guests with en-suite bathrooms, along with a small self-serve kitchen with a gallery. A modern wood heating system with a 70-kilowatt output and a 1,849-gal-

lon [7,000-liter] hot water tank provide the entire complex with heat and hot water. Filled with wood harvested from the property's own trees, the system heats the complex through the radiant floor heating installed on the ground level and through radiators on the upper levels.

Modern Ambiance and Mediterranean Flair

The vacation residence hall contains over 4,306 ft2 [400 m2] of floor space in total. The filigree precision of the structural details exudes a harmonious elegance that reveals itself already in the remarkable loggia, or recessed balcony, on the ground floor. French doors onto the terrace and floor-to-ceiling windows with decorative safety railings create a Mediterranean flair and let lots of light into the already bright and friendly interior. Sliding wooden window shutters on tracks underscore the building's sunny, lighthearted vacation atmosphere and the diagonal lines of their plank infills break up the strict symmetry of the façade. The flat hip roof lets the top floor enjoy high ceilings while it crowns the entire compact building with a 3.28' [1 meter] roof overhang to create a kind of roof canopy. This prototype is proof that a modern, solid wood house can be built on-site, using locally harvested wood from mixed and hardwood forests to create a healthy living environment. ●

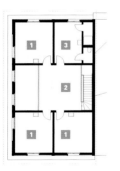

M 1:300
3RD FLOOR
1 ROOM
2 GALLERY
3 BATH/TOILETS

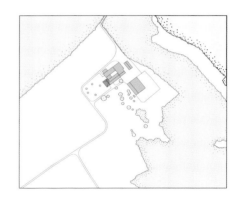

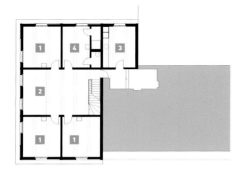

M 1:300
2ND FLOOR
1 ROOM
2 LIVING
3 KITCHEN
4 BATH

M 1:300
BASEMENT LEVEL
1 NATURAL CELLAR
2 STORAGE
3 UTILITY/MECHANICAL
4 TOILETS

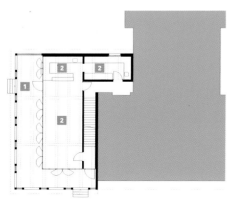

M 1:300
GROUND LEVEL
1 LOGGIA/PORCH
2 MULTI-FUNCTIONAL
 ROOM

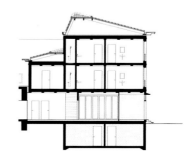

M 1:300 / **CROSS SECTION**

ℹ️ A total of approximately **4,856 ft³ [137.5 m³]** of wood volume was used in construction. This is equivalent to a carbon component in wood of **37.5 tons [34 metric tons]**, which is equivalent, in turn, to the storage of **137 tons [124 metric tons]** of carbon dioxide for 100 years.

ARCHITECT	BERNATH + WIDMER, ARCHITEKTEN ETH HTL SIA
CONSTRUCTION	BRÄDÄX BLOCKBAUZIMMEREI + BERGAUER HOLZBAU GMBH
LOCATION	SWITZERLAND, CANTON OF SCHAFFHAUSEN
LOT SIZE	746,929 FT², OR 17.14 ACRES [69,392 M²]
LIVING AREA	3,369 FT² [313 M²]
CONSTRUCTION COST	1,727,600 [1,234,000 EURO]
	BASED OF CALCULATION: 1 EURO = $1.40 USD
COMPLETION	2010

↑ Functional elegance is no contradiction in this bright wood building.

↑ As if country school residence halls always have to be dark, narrow, and dull: An inviting space for group dynamics under the gallery.

↓ Architectural playfulness and transparency make for great gatherings with this multifunctional room design.

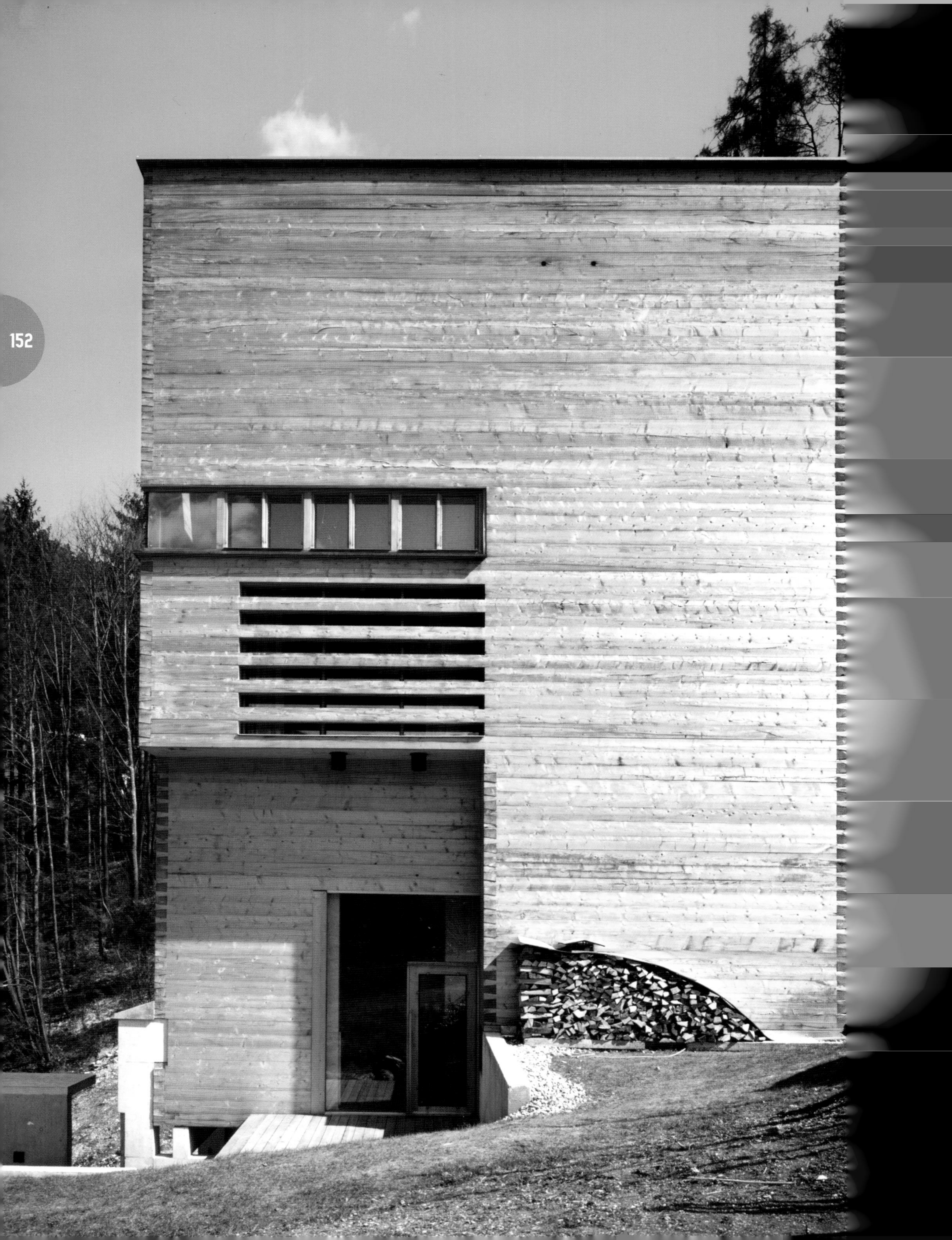

ONE-ROOM LOG TOWER

In Tyrol, Austria, not far from the provincial capital of Innsbruck, a log construction monument, visible from afar, shows the variety and modernity of solid wood construction.

Above the Inn Valley stands a log house on a 35-degree steep mountain slope near the entrance to the Alpbachtal, which forms a side valley following the course of the Alpbach stream. Because of the rocky and steep conditions of the building lot, the ground-plan area was conceived for a financially and structurally feasible foundation measuring exactly 20.34' x 27.6' [6.2 x 8.4 m]. The lot, which slopes down steeply to the northwest, determined the need to build vertically rather than horizontally. A vertical solid wood structure would, moreover, allow the upper level at least to avoid remaining completely in the shadow of the neighboring mountain peaks during the winter—at least for a few hours a day. Three full stories of living space were placed on top of a foundation of reinforced concrete in traditional one-shell log construction but in the unconventional form of a tower with an impressive total height of 49.2' [15 m]. Of course, the building plans were also heavily influenced by design considerations and the desire to keep the views from the lot open and unobstructed.

"Tiroler Schloss" or Tyrolean Lock Notches
The load-bearing log walls are 6.3" [16 cm] thick and were joined with a regionally traditional dovetail notch known as the Tiroler Schloss or Tyrolean lock. The centuries-old name originates in the old carpentry traditions of the Austrian, alpine province of the same name. This flush, high-quality notch type requires a great deal of carpentry skill and experience. It gives the log wall corners their eye-catchingly beautiful pattern. Before construction began,

← The unfussy, clean lines of the single-shell log tower of solid, planed fir wood with Tiroler Schloss notches.

the wood was dried in a kiln to a residual moisture content of fifteen percent. On the basis of a calculated measurement of .79" [2 cm] of projected settling per 3.24' [1 m] of height, all connections, doors, and windows were built separately to ensure a little leeway and sufficient settling space. In order to structurally counteract the force of the wind at higher levels, the posts from the basement to the roof were bound together with special steel threaded rods. Another stabilization measure was to notch the wood ceiling into the log house construction and bolt it to the walls.

Open Concept in a Vertical Structure
The concrete basement level of the log house provides space for a bathroom with a sauna as well as a large storage room for firewood. On the first floor, following long-standing tradition, there is a living room with a comfortable Stube, or family sitting room, with impressively high ceilings of 16.4' [5 m]. The other stories have ceiling heights of 11.5' [3.5 m], except for the children's room/floor with its much lower ceilings of 6.6' [2 m]—historically traditional for a log house. From the ground level, a stairway leads to a half-story, or mezzanine, where the kitchen with its gallery and open fireplace that exudes a cozy peacefulness is located. The level above the mezzanine houses the children's rooms, followed by the master bedroom on the fourth floor, and finally the terrace garden on the roof. Throughout the one-room log tower, oak and Swiss pine wood floors were installed. This home proves that open concept design is not just reserved for horizontally laid out floor plans, but works just as well for houses with a vertical layout.

Two Masonry Heaters
The components for the utilities in this log home were bundled into a compact installation channel that runs through the structure. In this one channel, next to the fireplace, are

← Consistent execution is evident in the interior as well. Wood dominates the form, look, feel, and smell of the house.

→ Large glass surfaces were deliberately left out of the design. The openings in the log tower façade, as well as the layout and lighting of the rooms, were executed with thoughtful reductionism.

↓ The kitchen mezzanine acts as a functional connector between the living area and the bedrooms.

→ The healthy log house climate and the minimal lighting in the bedroom promise restful nights.

all of the utility installations for water, electricity, and heat. Two masonry heaters built by a master craftsman heat the home with rated outputs of 8 and 6 kilowatts. Hot water is provided by an electric hot water heater as well as a solar unit with just 86 square feet [8 square meters] of flat plate collectors. On average, a total of approximately 49 cubic feet [15 cubic meters] of beech wood is needed to heat the one-room tower house for a year. The preservation of cultural identities and the focus on creating a natural living environment without chemicals, artificial foils, and insulation are perfectly reflected in the timeless architecture of this log house. ●

CONCEPT, SYSTEM-DEVELOPMENT + ARCHITECT	ARCHITEKT D.I. ANTONIUS LANZINGER
CONSTRUCTION	ZIMMEREI JOHANN PFISTER
LOCATION	AUSTRIA, TYROL
LOT SIZE	790 M² (8,503.5 FT², OR .20 ACRES)
LIVING AREA	135 M² (1,453 FT²)
CONSTRUCTION COST	NOT SPECIFIED
COMPLETION	2003

M 1:200
MEZZANINE
1 KITCHEN
2 GALLERY

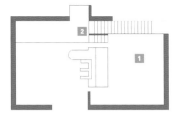

i A total of approximately **3,001.7 ft³ [85 m³]** of wood volume was used in construction. This is equivalent to a carbon component in wood of **23.1 tons [21 metric tons]**, which is equivalent, in turn, to the storage of **84.9 tons [77 metric tons]** of carbon dioxide for 100 years.

M 1:200
FIRST FLOOR
1 LIVING/FAMILY ROOM
2 BATH

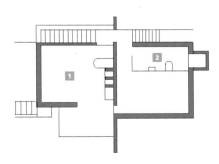

M 1:200
THIRD FLOOR
1 MASTER BEDROOM

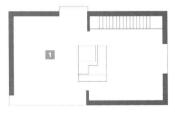

M 1:200
SECOND FLOOR
1 CHILDREN'S BEDROOM

M 1:200
BASEMENT
1 SAUNA
2 BATH
3 WOOD STORAGE

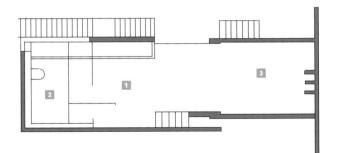

NEW PATHS FOR WOOD HOUSES

Years of experience in precision machinery fabrication for the wood industry formed the foundation of expertise for a revolutionary concept in solid wood construction.

Because of his deep insight into the lumber branch, this machinery and plant installer knew that the wood left over from the production of beams—the lumber edge cut from the solid slab—would be well-suited for creating a solid wood structure made of industrially pre-fabricated solid wood modules.

Perfect Pre-Fabrication

From simple boards of spruce, pine, fir, and Douglas fir of regional origin, completely pre-fabricated, serial wall elements are produced on a fully automated assembly line without chemical additives or glues. To begin with, the wood is dried to a residual moisture of fifteen percent so that it is dimensionally stable and resistant to pest infestation. In the next step, the .9" [23 mm] thick boards are grooved, creating an air pocket that will later improve the already outstanding insulating property of solid wood. Afterward, the boards are pressed together crosswise layer by layer. Small, diagonally arranged aluminum pins hold the individual boards together, producing great stability in the system elements. With this wall construction, later problems with settling, swelling, and shrinkage can be avoided. Measuring as much as 13.38" [34 cm] in thickness with fifteen layers, these system elements made of lumber-core plywood can be pre-fabricated. In the last step, the factory cuts the solid wood building components precisely to the millimeter and creates the recesses for electrical and sanitary systems and the openings for doors and windows.

Layer of Still Air

Despite the fact that the components are pre-fabricated at the factory, all of the advantages of solid-wood construction with regard to ecological building, environmen-

tal responsibility, and interior climate are conserved. The modules are moisture-regulating, dry, stable, sustainable, capable of sorption and storing, insulating, and extremely energy-saving in their production. Another process completes the well-conceived system: wax, sawdust, and sunflower oil are mixed together to create a wood mortar that is spread on all of the faces and joints of the individual wall parts. This unique mixture protects the construction elements from moisture and seals the grooved board layers to make them air-tight. This last advantage is particularly important because it creates the layers of still air in the solid wood components that are necessary for optimizing their insulating properties. The building elements can then be finished with wood paneling or plastered.

Variable and Time-saving Construction Method

The factory production system opens up a wide range of architectural and design options, beginning with flexible planning for the floor plan. Customized designs and multi-story, solid wood buildings can be executed without a problem. This stable and solid wall construction system makes it possible to utilize a variety of ceiling systems, for example joints for exposed ceiling constructions or alternative laminate timber ceilings that can also be pre-fabricated in the factory. Furthermore, the system, because of its massive, precise, and solid construction, has an above-average rating for soundproofing and fire prevention. The computerized production is not only exact but also time-saving: assembling a pre-fabricated wood house, includ-

↗ Sustainable combination of renewable raw materials and renewable energy: the solid wood house maximizes solar power.

→ The exterior cladding of the energy-plus house made of weatherproof larch wood will gray over time but will remain just as effective.

ing the roof truss, on top of an existing foundation only takes about three days. The components are put in place with a crane and then bolted together. After this, the interior construction can proceed as planned, on time and in logical progression—keeping cost calculations realistic.

An Energy-Plus House of Solid Wood

The wall construction of this one-and-a-half story house consists of a 13.4" [34 cm] thick wood wall system made of spruce and silver fir, followed by a 3.1" [8 cm] layer of soft wood fiber insulation, a ventilation layer, and a .9" [2.4 cm] thick outer layer of weatherproof larch cladding.

A brine-to-water heat pump with a rated capacity of 21 kilowatts provides the house with heat and hot water. Emissions-free, self-renewing, and cost-free geothermal heat is tapped through a collector system installed in the home's garden at a depth of 3.93' [1.2 m]. Low-energy wall and floor heating systems circulate the heat throughout the house. The photovoltaic system on the roof, extending over an area of 538 square feet [50 square meters] and with a peak performance of 13.3 kilowatts produces more electricity than the heat pump needs. The overall result: an exemplary energy-plus house made of solid wood, not foil and synthetic insulation materials. •

↓ The living room, with its wood stove and exposed beam ceiling, features larch wood parquet floors and contrasting white plaster walls.

ℹ A total of approximately **4,944 ft³ [140 m³]** of wood volume was used in construction. This is equivalent to a carbon component in wood of **38.6 tons [35 metric tons]**, which is equivalent, in turn, to the storage of **141 tons [128 metric tons]** of carbon dioxide for 100 years.

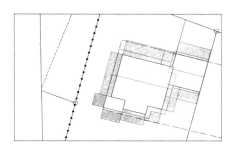

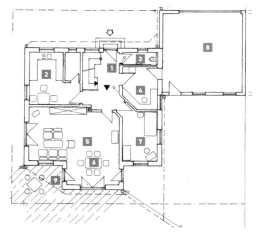

MANUFACTURER	MASSIV-HOLZ-MAUER ENTWICKLUNGS GMBH
ARCHITECT-CONCEPT	CH. D'ANDRADE, AITRACH
ARCHITECT-SUBMISSION PLANS	MAYR & SONNTAG, LEGAU
LOCATION	GERMANY, BADEN-WÜRTTEMBERG
LOT SIZE	11,690 FT², OR .27 ACRE [1,086 M²]
LIVING AREA	1,744 FT² [162 M²]
CONSTRUCTION COST	$315,000 [225,000 EURO]
	BASE OF CALCULATION: 1 EURO = $1.40 USD
COMPLETION	2005

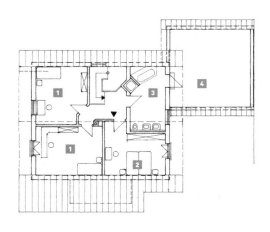

M 1:300 / **LOWER LEVEL**

1 ENTRY
2 KITCHEN
3 HALF-BATH
4 UTILITY/MECHANICAL
5 LIVING
6 DINING
7 GUEST ROOM
8 GARAGE
9 TERRACE

M 1:300 / **UPPER LEVEL**

1 BEDROOM
2 MASTER BEDROOM
3 BATH
4 STORAGE

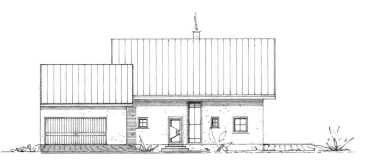

M 1:300 / **NORTH ELEVATION**

M 1:300 / **WEST ELEVATION**

↑ In the kitchen with its exposed beam ceiling, stone tiles were installed over the low-energy radiant floor heating system.

DREAM LOG HOUSE OF THE ARCTIC CIRCLE

In Western Ukraine, a Finnish log house on the edge of the Carpathian Mountains combines a thousand-year-old architectural culture with modern amenities.

The long experience and ancient tradition of the Finnish wood industry is evident in the manufacturer's sophisticated log house constructions. Because of the professional delivery of the individual building services, from the winter-felling of the wood, to its storage, the CAD planning and the computerized manufacturing, the kiln-drying to the assembly of the home, no work step in the complex process is left to chance. The manufacturer's own research department constantly aligns its findings to experience-based benchmarks and information garnered through international building projects. Only in this way was the Finnish log construction industry able to develop and perfect itself so that today it is capable of producing projects of the highest quality all over the world under the most varied climatic conditions. The integral construction system of the Finnish log house manufacturer combines efficiency and flexibility to create products of lasting value.

Laminated Logs of Polar Pine
The single-shell log house was built with squared off beams measuring 7.1" x 7.7" [18 x 19.5 cm]. In the world's largest log house manufacturing plant, not far from the Arctic Circle, log houses have always been built with polar pine. The slow-growing and highly prized "gold of the north" is cultivated and harvested with the greatest care in growth cycles projected for up to 150 years into the future in accordance with the principles of sustainable forestry. The wood is given the time it needs to mature and, thanks to its slow growth, its fibers attain their unique strength, hardiness, and durability. The triple laminated logs made of planed side-grain wood also allow for greater construction dimensioning. Moreover, the use of laminated wood prevents cracking, warping, and stronger settling tendencies in the load-bearing wood elements, whose weatherproof heartwood forms the wall's exterior side.

Center of Family Life with Bay Windows
The log house villa presents a clear and balanced form with its ground plan in the form of a cross, softened by three balcony terraces that wrap around the house. The rooms are laid out in the individual sections of the house to follow the path of the sun. Outside as well as inside, every eye is caught by the wall of glass rising to the roof ridge on the southeast gable. In the middle of this gable, a large bay window rises from the bottom of the building to extend over two stories, bringing more light and space to the rooms that form the center of family life in the log house. The form of the three-sided bay window is framed and accentuated by the projecting roof crowning the bay. On either side of the building's middle section with its impressive bay window, there is a gable-sided roofed extension: to the right, the stately main entrance and to the left, the south-facing terrace. The living room, open to the gallery above, is connected to but discreetly and formally separated from the adjacent dining room and kitchen areas as well as the utility and mechanical room.

↗ Stately but welcoming, thanks to the wood of the polar pine: the central main gable with its two-story bay window and the extensions to either side form the covered main entrance and the south terrace.

→ The garden-side area is a study in restraint with its emphasis on smaller but well-arranged accents.

↑ Openness and transparency characterize the flowing transitions of the individual rooms, whose solid wood log construction exudes calm and tranquility.

↑ The log house combines elegance and warmth to create its own cultivated atmosphere.

Balance and Flow

The lower level is completed by the office, a spacious bath with a Finnish sauna and its own small relaxation balcony, as well as a guest powder room. With their irregular black and white pattern, the gleaming stone tile floors of the ground level contrast dramatically with the solid wood walls. An L-shaped, solid wood stairway leads to the spacious gallery area on the upper level with its pine plank flooring. The three bedrooms for the children and their bathroom are accessible from the gallery. The luxurious master bedroom, the parents' own private refuge in the east wing of the upper level, features a huge walk-in closet. A masonry heater, centrally located in the living room, which is open to the roof ridge 26' [8 m] above, provides basic heat to the log house with its nominal output of 7 kilowatts. An economical gas-condensing combi-boiler helps meet the home's heating needs at peak times and provides hot water as well. Rooms are not strictly separated, but provide a functional delineation and order. ●

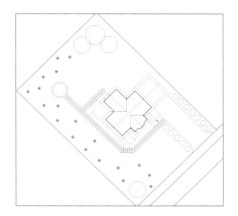

M 1:300 / **ELEVATION**

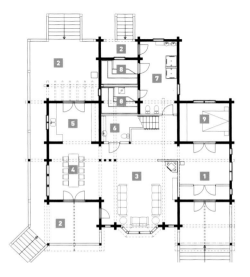

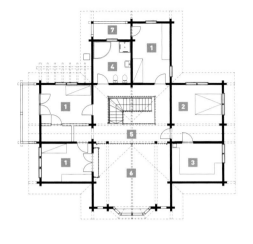

M 1:300
LOWER LEVEL

1 ENTRY
2 TERRACE
3 LIVING
4 DINING
5 KITCHEN
6 HALF-BATH
7 BATH
8 SAUNA
9 OFFICE/GUEST BEDROOM

M 1:300
UPPER LEVEL

1 BEDROOM—CHILD
2 MASTER BEDROOM
3 WALK-IN CLOSET
4 BATH
5 GALLERY
6 OPEN TO BELOW
7 BALCONY

i A total of approximately **6,886 ft³ [195 m³]** of wood volume was used in construction. This is equivalent to a carbon component in wood of **53.7 tons [48.7 metric tons]**, which is equivalent, in turn, to the storage of **196.2 tons [178 metric tons]** of carbon dioxide for 100 years.

MANUFACTURER + ARCHITECT	KONTIOTUOTE OY
LOCATION	UKRAINE
LOT SIZE	21,528 FT², OR .49 ACRE [2,000 M²]
LIVING AREA	2,648 FT² [246 M²]
CONSTRUCTION COST	$350,000 [250,000 EURO]
	BASE OF CALCULATION: 1 EURO = $1.40 USD
COMPLETION	2007

LOG HOUSE PALACE IN THE ROCKY MOUNTAINS

The grandfather restored palaces in old Berlin. The grandson, a descendant of German immigrants fulfills his own dream in Canada.

In the province of British Colombia, in the south of the Monashee mountain range in the Canadian Rockies, a unique and monumental log construction is perched at a lofty height of 6,652 feet [2,000 meters]. The imposing building is characterized by its expressively rich use of form. The Western Red Cedar from Pacific coastal regions is used so impressively in this construction that it dominates the strikingly stately scenery. The building's wide, sweeping, flying roof ridges and purlins call to mind images of fairy-tale worlds, which have been made real here. A striking tower that underscores the fairy-tale castle character of the chalet rises from its center. The tower acts as the central connecting passage in the two-story complex built in the post-and-beam mixed construction style.

A Conical Roof Like a Witch's Hat

The tower rests on a massive circular dry-stack stone foundation, that is, one made of irregularly sized stones stacked without mortar. In the center of the tower stands a western red cedar trunk with a height of about 46' [14 m], around which a solid wood stairway spirals upward with its floating handrail that seems to wind itself like a vine around the tree. The untreated, peeled tree trunk measures 4.9' [1.5 m] across at its base. Its massive upper end forms the base for the conical roof whose exposed beams seem to fan out around the spindle-like trunk. The conical roof that looks like a witch's hat from the outside has become the

emblem of the mountain chalet. A transept running from east to west builds the residential wing of the complex. From the transverse main body, large, gable-fronted annexes studded with many large windows extend along all sides of the building. To the south these extensions house the kitchen, the central living area, and a luxurious bedchamber.

One-of-a-kind Pieces as Far as the Eye Can See

Bronze-trimmed chandeliers, walls decorated with landscape and wildlife carvings, and hand-crafted solid wood doors with wrought-iron fittings in the interiors are examples of contemporary one-of-a-kind artisan craftsmanship. High-quality walnut parquet floors alternate with jet black volcanic stone flooring. Visitors will marvel at the wildly natural beds made of incredibly massive logs in the guest rooms that can be as much as 1,076 square feet [100 square meters] in size. The entire log building is artfully lit in large part with indirect LED lights. The dramatically exposed log supports and roof beams of fragrant western red cedar are the distinguishing feature of all of the rooms throughout the complex. All of the logs used in the chalet's construction were hand-picked, individually processed, and come—or better said were rescued—largely from areas that were damaged by storms, high winds, and forest fires.

The River of Life Springs from the Heart of the Log House

The stately entrance opens onto the seemingly endless expanses of the log house interior. In the middle of the floor springs the river of all life: a mosaic-like path created from glass, quartz, and mica meandering from the entrance area toward the Great Room. This piece of art embedded in the floor is a unique homage to the breathtaking beauty of North America. A cinema, a wellness area with a sauna, steam bath, and a spa are located on

↖ A structure like a natural phenomenon: the mountain chalet with its witch's hat tower lets the imagination roam free.

← Western red cedar shows its pure, primitive power and natural beauty as a building material.

← This interior design composition is unparalleled and calls up countless associations with its details.

→ The 46' [14 m] high natural trunk log seems like an axle in the middle of the tower with its exposed roof beams like the spokes of a wheel radiating from the conical roof.

the basement level. A rock garden of boulders edges the mountain chalet and secures the grounds like an oversized dry stone wall. Guests can ski right up to the door of this log house palace in the middle of one of Canada's most beautiful ski areas. Up to 24.6' [7.5 m] of the famous "champagne powder" snow falls here every year. The mountain chalet's energy needs are met by an emissions-free geothermal heating system, which feeds the low-energy radiant floor heating on all stories and provides hot water. Three of the four masonry heaters are connected to the central heating system in the building and all of them provide guests with unforgettable moments in the log house palace in the Canadian Rockies. ●

↑ Opulence and the thrill of anticipation—a good night's rest, newly defined.

MANUFACTURER	PIONEER LOG HOMES OF BRITISH COLUMBIA
ARCHITECT	DON GESINGER
LOCATION	CANADA, BRITISH COLUMBIA
LOT SIZE	13,124 FT2 [4,000 M2]
LIVING AREA	3050 FT2 [929 M2]
CONSTRUCTION COST	NOT SPECIFIED
COMPLETION	IN 2010

■ A total of approximately **86,521 ft³ [2,450 m³]** of wood volume was used in construction. This is equivalent to a carbon component in wood of **674.6 tons [612 metric tons]**, which is equivalent, in turn, to the storage of **2,476 tons [2,246 metric tons]** of carbon dioxide for 100 years.

↓ The river of all life springs from the middle of the log house and meanders to the center of the wide Great Room.

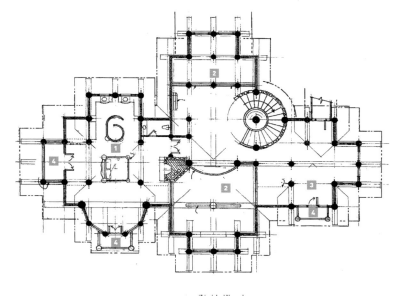

M 1:400
UPPER LEVEL
1 SUITE
2 OPEN TO BELOW
3 BALCONY
4 WORK/OFFICE

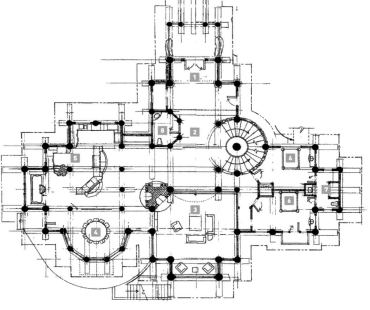

M 1:400
LOWER LEVEL

1	ENTRY	5	KITCHEN
2	RECEPTION	6	BEDROOM
3	GREAT ROOM	7	BATH
4	DINING	8	TOILET

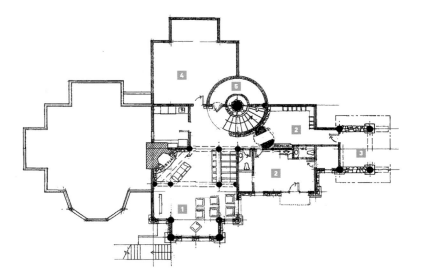

M 1:400
BASEMENT LEVEL
1 THEATER
2 WELLNESS AREA
3 STONE GARDEN
4 UTILITY/MECHANICAL
5 WINE CELLAR

MANUFACTURERS' CONTACTS

ARCHITECT D.I. ANTONIUS LANZINGER
M 9 ARCHITEKTEN
MARIA-THERESIEN-STRASSE 9
A-6020 INNSBRUCK, AUSTRIA
TEL.: +43 512 573198
WWW.M9-ARCHITEKTEN.AT
PAGE 152
PHOTOS: GÜNTER RICHARD WETT, INNSBRUCK, AUSTRIA

ARTIFEX GMBH
MOOSEURACH 22
D-82549 KÖNIGSDORF, GERMANY
TEL.: +49 8179 997286
WWW.ARTIFEX-BLOCKBAU.DE
PAGE 96
PHOTOS: ARGUM

BERNATH + WIDMER ARCHITEKTEN ETH HTL SIA
GIEBELSTRASSE 35
CH-8037 ZURICH, SWITZERLAND
TEL.: +41 44 2739010
PAGE 146
PHOTOS: © ROLAN BERNATH

BLOCKHAUSBAU PORRENGA GMBH
GEWERBESTRASSE 3
CH-8634 HOMBRECHTIKON, SWITZERLAND
TEL.: +41 55 2441606
WWW.BLOCKHAUSBAU.CH
PAGE 76

CHARLIE MANZ BLOCKHAUSBAU GMBH
P.O. BOX 1205
D-54494 MORBACH, GERMANY
TEL.: +49 6533 958862
WWW.CHARLIE-MANZ.DE
PAGE 100

CHIEMGAUER HOLZHAUS—LPS HOLZHAUS GMBH & CO. KG
SEIBOLDSDORFER MÜHLE 1 A
D-83278 TRAUNSTEIN, GERMANY
TEL.: +49 861 1661920
WWW.CHIEMGAUER-HOLZBAU.DE
PAGE 86

DANYS LOG HOME
WÜERIBÖDELI
CH-3753 OEY, SWITZERLAND
TEL.: +41 33 453 2007
WWW.DANYSLOGHOME.CH
PAGE 142

DAS HOLZHAUS OLIVER SCHATTAT GMBH
AUF DER LEHMKAUTE 4
D-63589 LINSENGERICHT GEISLITZ, GERMANY
TEL.: +49 6051 4747850
WWW.HOLZHAUS-GMBH.DE
PAGE 52

ELK-FERTIGHAUS AG
INDUSTRIESTRASSE 1
A-3943 SCHREMS, AUSTRIA
TEL.: +43 2853 705
WWW.ELK.AT
PAGE 46

FISCHER HOLZBAU GMBH
AM LEHMBERG 9
D-17166 HOHEN DEMZIN, GERMANY
TEL.: +49 3996 172088
WWW.ZEDERNHOLZHAUS.DE
PAGE 138

FLOSS ZIMMEREI UND BLOCKHAUSBAU GMBH
LINDENSTRASSE 20 B
D-54614 SCHÖNECKEN/EIFEL, GERMANY
TEL.: +49 6553 9208 0
WWW.FLOSS-HOLZBAU.DE
PAGE 82

FULLWOOD WOHNBLOCKHAUS GMBH
OBERSTE HÖHE
D-53797 LOHMAR, GERMANY
TEL.: +49 2206 9533 700
WWW.FULLWOOD.DE
PAGE 20

GEBRÜDER DUFTER GMBH
ZIMMEREI UND HOLZBEARBEITUNG
TRAUNSTEINER STRASSE 81
D-83334 INZELL, GERMANY
TEL.: +49 8665 1375
WWW.DUFTER-RUSTIKALE-HOLZBEARBEITUNG.DE
PAGE 104

GRAHAM BRUCE OFIELD
OVERFIELD NATURAL HOMES
DORFSTRASSE 23
D-54424 LÜCKENBURG, GERMANY
TEL.: +49 6504 950062
WWW.OFIELD.DE
PAGE 112

HOLZBAU MAIER GMBH & CO. KG
GEWERBESTRASSE 171
A-5733 BRAMBERG, AUSTRIA
TEL.: +43 6566 7264
WWW.MAIER.AT
PAGE 26

HOLZBAU ANDREAS VOLLMERS
MEISTERBETRIEB—ZIMMEREI UND BLOCKHAUSBAU
LÖHBERGERSTRASSE 11
D-21755 HECHTHAUSEN, GERMANY
TEL.: +49 4774 893
WWW.HOLZBAU-VOLLMERS.DE
PAGE 58
PHOTOS: KIRK DAHMKE, D-OTTERNDORF, GERMANY

HONKARAKENNE OYJ
LAHDENTIE 870
FIN-04401 JÄRVENPÄÄ, FINLAND
TEL.: +358 20 575700
WWW.HONKA.COM
PAGE 90

JOST NATURSTAMMHAUS
IN DER MESS 16
D-66620 NONNWEILER, GERMANY
TEL.: +49 6873 901665
WWW.STEFANJOST.DE
PAGE 38

KONTIOTUOTE OY
RANUANTIE 224
FIN-93100 PUDAS JÄRVI, FINLAND
TEL.: +358 20 770 7400
WWW.KONTIO.COM
PAGE 162

LÖFFLER NATURSTAMMHAUS GMBH & CO. KG
LIEBENSTEINER STRASSE 39
D-98599 BROTTERODE, GERMANY
TEL.: +49 36840 30760
WWW.LOEFFLER-NATURSTAMMHAUS.DE
PAGE 124

LOG BLOCKHAUS ING. THOMAS ZEILINGER GMBH
KREUZÄCKERWEG 3A
A-2485 WIMPASSING, AUSTRIA
TEL.: +43 664 5025108
WWW.LOGBLOCKHAUS.AT
PAGE 42

MARK MASSIVHOLZHAUS
NEUNKIRCHNER STRASSE 136
D-66557 ILLINGEN, GERMANY
TEL.: +49 6825 495183
WWW.MARK-MASSIVHOLZHAUS.DE
PAGE 32

MASSIV-HOLZ-MAUER ENTWICKLUNGS GMBH
AUF DER GEIGERHALDE 41
D-87459 PFRONTEN-WEISSBACH, GERMANY
TEL.: +49 8332 923319
WWW.MASSIVHOLZMAUER.DE
PAGE 158

NORDIC HAUS BLOCKHÄUSER
AM WEIHER 1
D-49439 STEINFELD
TEL.: +49 5492 7491
WWW.NORDIC-HAUS.DE
PAGE 108

PIONEER LOG HOMES OF BRITISH COLOMBIA
351 HODGSON ROAD
WILLIAMS LAKE BRITISH COLOMBIA
CANADA V2G 3P7
TEL.: +1 250 392 5577
WWW.PIONEERLOGHOMESOFBC.COM
PAGE 166

POLAR LIFE HAUS – HONKATALOT
KITULANMÄENTIE 42
FIN-63640 RITOLA – TOYSÄ / FINLAND
TEL.: +358 201 758500
WWW.POLARLIFEHAUS.COM
PAGE 64

REMS-MURR-HOLZHAUS GMBH
WIESENSTRASSE 9
D-71577 GROSSERLACH-GRAB, GERMANY
TEL.: +49 7192-20244
WWW.REMSMURR-HOLZHAUS.DE
PAGE 130

RUBNER HAUS AG
HANDWERKERZONE 4
1-39030 KIENS / SÜDTIROL, ITALY
TEL.: +39 0474 563333
WWW.HAUS.RUBNER.COM
PAGE 70
PHOTOS: RUBNER HAUS AG

TEAM KANADABLOCKHAUS GMBH
MARKSTRASSE 3
D-71540 MURRHARDT, GERMANY
TEL.: +49 7192 935970
WWW.KANADABLOCKHAUS.DE
PAGE 118

VINZENZ BACHMANN
RAITENER STRASSE 17
D-83259 SCHLECHING-METTENHAM, GERMANY
TEL.: +49 8649 9880 0
WWW.VINZENZ-BACHMANN.DE
PAGE 134

COPYRIGHT

174

ISBN: 978-0-7643-4330-8
Printed in China

Published by Schiffer Publishing, Ltd.
4880 Lower Valley Road
Atglen, PA 19310
Phone: (610) 593-1777; Fax: (610) 593-2002
E-mail: Info@schifferbooks.com

For the largest selection of fine reference books on this and related subjects, please visit our website at **www.schifferbooks.com.** You may also write for a free catalog.

This book may be purchased from the publisher.
Please try your bookstore first.

We are always looking for people to write books on new and related subjects. If you have an idea for a book, please contact us at
proposals@schifferbooks.com

Schiffer Books are available at special discounts for bulk purchases for sales promotions or premiums. Special editions, including personalized covers, corporate imprints, and excerpts can be created in large quantities for special needs. For more information contact the publisher.

In Europe, Schiffer books are distributed by
Bushwood Books
6 Marksbury Ave.
Kew Gardens
Surrey TW9 4JF England
Phone: 44 (0) 20 8392 8585; Fax: 44 (0) 20 8392 9876
E-mail: info@bushwoodbooks.co.uk
Website: www.bushwoodbooks.co.uk

Other Schiffer Books on Related Subjects:
Cedar Style: A Look at Lovely Log Homes.
Tina Skinner & Roger Wade. ISBN: 978-0-7643-2951-7. $39.95
Log Cabins: Past & Present.
Tina Skinner & Tommi Jamison. ISBN: 978-0-7643-3013-1. $34.99

This book was originally published as *BLOCKHÄUSER: Massive Holzhäuser zum Wohnen und Leben* by Verlag Georg D.W. Callwey GmbH & Co.KG in 2010. The original ISBN number was 978-3-7667-1855-6.

Translated by Omicron Language Solutions, LLC

ALL PHOTOGRAPHS AND PLANS WERE KINDLY PROVIDED BY THE MANUFACTURERS FOR THIS PUBLICATION, UNLESS OTHERWISE NOTED.

SOURCES AND PHOTO CREDITS:
PAGE 9: PFAHLBAUMUSEUM (STILT HOUSE MUSEUM) UNTER-UHLDINGEN, GERMANY; **PAGE 10 TOP:** HAGEN RÜGER, ERLICH-THOF RIETSCHEN; **PAGE 10 BOTTOM:** DIREKTORENWOHNHAUS (DIRECTOR'S RESIDENCE) NIESKY, ARCHITECT KONRAD WACHS-MANN, EXECUTION CHRISTOPH & UNMACK AG, NIESKY/OL, 1927, ARCHIVE MUSEUM NIESKY; **PAGE 14 (BOTH IMAGES):** ARTI-FEX GMBH; **PAGE 17 (BOTH ILLUSTRATIONS):** WWW.CO2-BANK. DE, **COVER PICTURE:** RUBNER HAUS AG

With the kind support of
Brunner ®
Wood heating systems for masonry heaters and fireplaces.
www.brunner.de

MAFI
Walk on art